KNIGHT-CAPRON LIBRARY
LYNCHBURG COLLEGE
LYNCHBURG, VIRGINIA

WITHDRAWN

Stella Benson

Twayne's English Authors Series

Kinley E. Roby, Editor
Northeastern University

TEAS 359

KNIGHT-CAPRON LIBRARY
LYNCHBURG COLLEGE
LYNCHBURG, VIRGINIA 24501

Stella Benson

By R. Meredith Bedell

Virginia Military Institute

Twayne Publishers • Boston

PR
6003
. E72
Z58
1983

Stella Benson

R. Meredith Bedell

Copyright © 1983 by G. K. Hall & Company
All Rights Reserved
Published by Twayne Publishers
A Division of G. K. Hall & Company
70 Lincoln Street
Boston, Massachusetts 02111

Book Production by John Amburg
Book Design by Barbara Anderson

Printed on permanent/durable acid-free
paper and bound in the United States of
America.

Library of Congress Cataloging in Publication Data

Bedell, R. Meredith.
Stella Benson.

(Twayne's English authors series; TEAS 359)
Bibliography: p. 133
Includes index.
1. Benson, Stella, 1892–1933
—Criticism and interpretation.   I. Title.   II. Series.
PR6003.E72Z58   1983   823.'912   82-23223
ISBN   0-8057-6845-9

for Elery M. and Ruth T. Zehner

Contents

About the Author
Preface
Chronology

    Chapter One
    Times and Places   1

    Chapter Two
    The Singular Voice   16

    Chapter Three
    Public Facade and Private Identity   24

    Chapter Four
    The Novels of Fantasy   40

    Chapter Five
    Living in the Real World   62

    Chapter Six
    Exiles and Émigrés   85

    Chapter Seven
    Arrangements and Collections   111

    Chapter Eight
    Conclusion   122

Appendix   127
Notes and References   129
Selected Bibliography   133
Index   139

About the Author

With a B.A. in Political Science from Wake Forest College and a Ph.D. in English from Florida State University, Meredith Bedell is now an associate professor of English at the Virginia Military Institute. She has also taught at Florida State University and in a migrant education program in Pahokee and Belle Glade, Florida.

Preface

The American novelist Ida A. Wylie once remarked that

> The English are a strange people. They seem so unromantic, so carefully commonplace and stiffly formalized. Then suddenly out of the apparently stagnant waters of their conformity they throw up these Lawrences . . . and Stella Bensons. Sometimes I suspect that they are a nation of eccentrics, cautiously concealing their eccentricity and that once in a while, sometimes in the hour of the country's desperate need one of them breaks loose.[1]

Stella Benson began her first novel in 1912, a time when her country, if not the world, stood in desperate need of something to hold on to. When Queen Victoria died on January 22, 1901, she left her name upon an age and had imprinted the conventions of her attitudes upon a people. Queen of England, Empress of India, sovereign of an empire upon which the sun never set, Victoria had believed women should stay in the home and obey their husbands. However, by the time of her death God in His heaven seemed in danger of permanent eclipse, and women were climbing down off pedestals. Quite literally, there was little on earth or elsewhere that seemed secure. Victorianism, whatever *that* really was,[2] had been on the wane for some time. The evangelical fervor that had accompanied the inauguration of Victoria's reign appeared to have become an ossified sense of propriety; moral values became social decorum. But decorum was no defense against a changing world. As the twentieth century moved into its second decade, automobiles, which were little more than seldom-seen curiosities ten years earlier, had become a relative commonplace. Airplanes crossed the sky and soon became not merely curiosities but fearful instruments of death. As science seemed to gain importance there were dismayed attempts to withdraw from a reality often seen as hopelessly deterministic, pushed along with nearly incomprehensible scientific advances. This was the age of Stella Benson: an age marked by disillusion, despair, hope, and idealism.

Born in 1892 before the horrors of modern warfare were imagined and the might of England had been seriously challenged, Stella Benson died in 1933 deploring what she called the disease of imitation-life and mindless values. During those forty-one years nearly every thought that man had ever had was questioned; answers were tenuous, temporary, and troubling. R. Ellis Roberts in *Portrait of Stella Benson* said of her:

> She was herself acutely aware of the period, of her generation—as aware as D. H. Lawrence or Aldous Huxley: and she is more representative of that generation because she was, in her bones, more a child of tradition, and so felt more violently the huge break in tradition that occurred in her lifetime. . . . The value of her work as a mirror of her generation's desires and losses and torments consists in the truth that she was essentially ordinary, typically English and therefore eccentric.[3]

Stella Benson is representative of her age in the concern she felt for the problems in the world around her and the dismay with which she evaluated solutions. The objective of this study is to trace the transmutations of the recurring subject of Benson's novels: the isolation that characterizes the human condition. Her recognition of the fundamentally solitary plight of the individual came early in her work, but her response to the situation gradually changed. Her novels move from a concern for the plight of the individual and a criticism of the inadequacy of society in general and usual methods of communication in particular, to a hesitant, tentative examination of whatever may be positive in an admittedly less-than-perfect world. She attempted to discern what is unique in an individual, indeed what constitutes an individual, and then to discover some manner of treaty through which the individual may cope with a fundamentally alien surrounding world.

The first chapter of this study is a fairly comprehensive biographical sketch. There are two reasons for taking the time and space for the detailed biography in what is essentially a critical examination of an author's works. In the first place, the details of Benson's life are not generally known. The only biography of Stella Benson, R. Ellis Roberts's *Portrait of Stella Benson*, is out of print, is poorly documented, cites passages from her fiction to support his suppositions (which are usually presented as fact), and is by Roberts's own admission incomplete. Although I have used his book for general biographical information, the first chapter is not simply a condensation of his work but a new study drawing heavily upon unpublished letters written by Benson herself. The second reason for including this biographical chapter is to point the way to another type of study. As most writers, Benson drew upon her own life and experiences for much of the material in her fiction as well as her nonfiction work. A study of Benson's work as a reflection of and

Preface

transformation of personal experience would certainly be interesting but does not fall within the scope of this particular study.

The remaining chapters are a critical examination of Stella Benson's literary works. Chapter 2 offers an overview of Benson's work, commenting on her technique and themes and comparing these to other works of the time. Chapters 3 through 6 examine the themes found in the individual novels and consider the changes in perspective and treatment found in the works themselves. Because these novels are out of print and not always available in local libraries, I have preceded the analysis of each novel with a brief plot summary and have quoted liberally. Chapter 7 is devoted to Benson's short stories, poems, and nonfiction, and Chapter 8 to general concluding comments and an assessment of her place in English literature.

While I have been working on this book I have received assistance and encouragement from many people. My thanks go to all of them, but I do particularly want to thank Dr. Fred Standley of Florida State University for his guidance and encouragement early in the study and the Virginia Military Institute for summer grants in support of my research. I also wish to thank Mrs. Georgina Berkeley, Stella Benson's literary executor, for permission to quote from published and unpublished sources. Finally, but most important, I must thank my family: my husband Robert for his critical reading, wholehearted support and infinite patience, and my children Marty, Scott, and Ethan for their distractions and understanding.

R. Meredith Bedell

Virginia Military Institute

Chronology

1892	Stella Benson born January 6, in Shropshire, England, to Caroline Essex Cholmondeley and Ralph Beaumont Benson.
1899	Death of her sister Catherine.
1901	Begins lifelong practice of writing a diary.
1910	In Switzerland for a sinus operation; one result of the operation was permanent partial deafness. Begins to be drawn into the feminist movement.
1912	On the return voyage of a cruise to Jamaica begins her first novel.
1913	Moves to London and holds a succession of jobs to support herself.
1915	*I Pose*.
1917	*This Is the End*.
1918	*Twenty*; first trip to the United States: July, arrived in New York; December, arrived in California.
1919	*Living Alone*.
1920	Travelled in China and India; September, met Shaemas (James) O'Gorman Anderson in Chungking.
1921	Returned to England; September 29, married Anderson, a Chinese customs official; October, left with husband for second trip to California.
1922	*The Poor Man*; *Kwan-Yin*; May–October, visited Andersons in Ireland; October, left for Mengtsz, China.
1924	*Pipers and a Dancer*.
1925	*The Little World*; *The Awakening*; Andersons transferred to Shanghai; Benson spends summer in California, rejoins husband in Lung Ching Tsun.
1926	*Goodbye, Stranger*.
1927	December, 1926–March, 1927 visits California.
1927–1929	Andersons take two-year leave in Europe and England.

1928	*Worlds Within Worlds*; *The Man Who Missed the Bus*.
1929	Anderson reassigned to Nanning, China.
1930	Andersons rescued from besieged city of Nanning, assigned to Hong Kong.
1931	*Tobit Transplanted* (in the U.S. *The Far Away Bride*); *Hope Against Hope and Other Stories*.
1932	*Christmas Formula and Other Stories*; January—August visit to California and England.
1933	*Pull Devil, Pull Baker*; died December 6.
1935	*Mundos: an Unfinished Novel*; *Poems*.
1936	*Collected Short Stories*.

Chapter One
Times and Places
England and the World: 1892–1921

Stella Benson was born on January 6, 1892, at Lutwyche Hall in Shropshire, England. This Elizabethan mansion, built in 1581, had been the Benson family residence for over one hundred years. Though there had been remodelling activities since the original construction, Lutwyche was a cold home in the winter, high on a hill overlooking the ocean. Stella was the third of four children from the marriage of Ralph Beaumont Benson and Caroline Essex Cholmondeley, sister of the successful novelist Mary Cholmondeley. Benson money came from the Indies, a fact which haunted Ralph Beaumont Benson, a strict disciplinarian, a man driven by "an obscure passion to compensate in some way for the suffering which he knew must have been caused by the methods which had collected the Benson fortune."[1] Mr. Benson was often absent from home; however, Caroline Benson was not left to care for her family singlehandedly. A series of "nanas" helped direct the activities of the Benson children, and as might be expected in light of the father's disposition, these women were not usually lax with their charges. One, a crusading soldier in the Salvation Army, was so zealous in her recruiting efforts that she won a temporary convert in the child Stella Benson, but an implacable foe in the woman Stella Benson was to become. The intensity of Benson's disapproval of the pious moral rectitude displayed by these protectors of children is reflected in an article she wrote at a time when the Germans and English had been slaughtering each other for four years. "Almost all that is reactionary in England, I think, may be traced to the influence of Nana. . . . I like to think of the Kaisers and the Nanas of the world crumbling in a common ruin. Just as the Kaiser has given democracy a greater impetus than it ever had before, so such Nanas as mine have, in their homely way, done more toward the saving of souls than they knew."[2] When, as an adult, Stella arrived in the United States, she found the freedom allowed the young remarkable. Although she did not care for the American youth once he began to "adolesce," she announced her intention to subscribe to the American child-rearing method while her children (if she should have any) were young.

Benson was, no doubt, right in her belief that her childhood was bounded by restrictions. However, the control was not simply a convenience or convention; it was a physical necessity, for she was plagued with bronchial problems her entire life. Her sister had died when Stella was seven, and her parents were understandably concerned about the delicate health of their remaining daughter. Even at home with private instruction her health would break, and Mrs. Benson would take her daughter to a healthier climate for recuperation.

With a noted authoress for an aunt and a mother whose imagination could produce a story on demand with no apparent effort, it is not surprising that this girl, unable to run freely in a cold outdoors which could attack her lungs and sinuses, would turn to writing. She was contributing to the children's pages of the journal *St. Nicholas* when she was seven years old, and in 1901, at the age of nine, she began making entries in a diary, a practice she was to continue until she died.

When she was eighteen her health seemed to be improving, so in 1910 she went to Freiburg, Germany, to study music and to learn French and German. Unfortunately, within a month her health broke again, and she went to Switzerland to recuperate, a process that eventually required a painful operation to correct a disabling sinus condition. Although the operation lessened her pain, it did not prevent a permanent loss of hearing. During her eighteen-month convalescence at Arosa, Switzerland, Benson's health improved and her interests broadened. She was exposed to and subscribed to the feminist position that was being so forcefully advocated in England at that time. Rebellious urges were moving her toward an assertion of independence, but the break did not come at once. As a final effort for Stella's recovery, Mrs. Benson took her daughter on a cruise to Jamaica. In 1912, on the return voyage from Mandeville, Jamaica, Stella Benson was writing her first novel.

Mrs. Benson's intentions were, no doubt, to have her daughter return from Jamaica improved in health and ready to reenter the protective fold of Lutwyche. Her daughter, however, had other ideas. In 1913, at the age of twenty-one, over her mother's objections, she asserted her independence by moving to London. The decision to leave home and live in London might alarm any mother with a child whose health seemed so precariously maintained. However, Benson's decision produced increased alarm because she set up her headquarters in Hoxton, an area in London well known for its poverty and violence, but known also for its gaiety, carousing, and cockney spirit. So Stella Benson, writer, worker, suffragette, set out to see the world, the world of London.

The free spirit seemed to be not only what she wanted but what she needed. Not until 1916 did she have another serious illness; the working life and independence seemed to agree with her. London was the place for writers to be, and Benson considered herself a writer. But already at work in her was a recognition of reality, a practicality reflecting a lifelong desire to be financially independent. She did not set out for London with the intention of starving in some garret until her writing supported her. She first found a job with the Charity Organization Society, but she soon became disenchanted with the attitude and methods of that organization. When World War I began, she left the Society and became a secretary. In addition to pursuing this form of conventional employment, she was engaged in other independent enterprises. She rented a room and went into partnership with a crippled woman to make paper bags; she also embarked on her own private vocational training program—teaching anyone who wished to learn the intricacies of basket weaving. This last project ended as the students gained enough expertise to work alone or wandered back to being street vendors.[3] During what ever spare time she had, or could insist upon, Benson was writing. *I Pose*, her first novel, was published in 1915 by Macmillan and Company, the company which was publishing the novels of her aunt, Mary Cholmondeley. In 1917 her second novel, *This Is the End*, was published, to be followed one year later by *Twenty*, a volume of poetry. In the meantime she worked as a professional jobbing gardener, became a farm laborer, worked to improve the conditions of life for prostitutes, and withstood the onslaught of romantic importunity.

While freedom might have been what she was seeking, and Hoxton and then farm work certainly offered a type of freedom not to be found within the solicitous confines of Lutwyche, Benson noticed around her the strict limitations, physical and mental, imposed by poverty. These limitations were more ironclad than familial overprotection of the frail in health could ever be. Her disillusionment is reflected in the conclusion of an article she wrote about her experiences in the "Brown Borough" (Hoxton): "The march of civilization is not a particularly well-organized procession: sometimes it almost seems as if the stragglers outnumber those who keep in step. . . . In the van of the march the music brays confidently, wearying the ears of heaven with its brazen boastings of progress. . . . Perhaps Heaven only hears the boasting, perhaps Heaven has washed its hands of us, perhaps after all we are but dirt and deserve nothing better."[4] This bitter comment, containing within it the hope that this dreary view is not in fact the case, reveals Benson's central concern in her life and her work. What does one do when one suspects that all is *not* right with the world? How does one respond to the growing conviction that both racial progress and individual worth are empty phrases, not even credible illusions?

The war was an inescapable fact of life for the people of England, and it affected even those not directly involved. Although neither of Benson's brothers was killed (both were in the army), the carnage of the conflict confronted her everywhere: the despair of widows and families of the dead, the reality of maimed survivors, the scarcity of un-uniformed able-bodied men, and the scarcity of consumer goods. As the mud of Europe reddened with blood and the war which was supposed to end quickly dragged on for years, many sensitive people did look with wonder at the size of the toll exacted by international politics. Stella Benson revealed her own anguish when she recorded the cry of Mrs. MaryAnn, who expressed an approved "detached and sober sympathy with the allies," although behind her business-as-usual facade she felt the politics in human terms: "'Bill's boy gawn . . .' she said. 'All the chaps gawn. English or German—it don't seem to make no difference. By Gawd it's got to be a pretty fair peace, for to make this 'ere War worth while.'"[5]

Depressed by the reality of war-wracked England, and in spite of her mother's objections, Benson sailed from Liverpool for New York on July 8, 1918, to see the world and strengthen her lungs in the Colorado and California sun. She arrived in New York armed with determination and letters of introduction. After being lonely for almost one whole day, she was caught up in the life first of New York and then of Radnor, Pennsylvania. By the time she reached Chicago she was, as Harriet Monroe, editor of *Poetry: A Magazine of Verse*, described her, "a wisp of a girl . . . so pale and thin that we thought she must be either ill or starving, and feared she would collapse. . . . She was a weird and eerie little creature, frail in body but possessed of a keen mind, a roving imagination and an indomitable will."[6] The indomitable will was exercised as the frail young woman set out for the Colorado sun—in November, 1918. She was welcomed to Colorado not by a warm sun but by snow. "I was laid up directly I arrived, as we had a heavy snow and frost which proved a little too rigorous for a newcomer with only an outdoor porch to sleep on. However, a porch is a thankless place to be ill on, so I have struggled up to-day."[7] She finally arrived in Berkeley, California, on December 21, 1918.

Her hostess-to-be, Bertha Pope, was ill with influenza in Pennsylvania, so Benson, a newcomer in California, awaited her arrival in her empty house, alone and without friends for two weeks. When Mrs. Pope finally arrived there began a social whirl which, by the end of January, 1919, caused Benson to observe, "I seem to be a changed woman in this country. The very air is irresponsible, and the sun undiluted makes you drunk. My hair-shirt is temporarily laid aside, and I am glad to see—for once in a rather morbid life—this life that happy people live in the sun."[8] But the euphoria was short-lived. Less than a month later she wrote: "I am becoming a very old worried woman, and in a way very lonely—I feel as if I were dead—me, I mean, the me that people might like, or be interested in not only as a foothold or a tearbottle, but as a *me*. I do not know what happened to me. . . . I think somehow I forgot to be born alive, and now among these passionate and hysterically alive Californians, I noticed it unmistakeably for the first time. . . ."[9] She overworked and overpartied and in April succumbed to pleurisy and its demands for professional attention. She did not rest for long; she was out of the hospital in May and matching the frenetic pace set by her California friends.

In September, 1919, she co-founded a Poetry Club and in December admitted "I seem to have got the hang of California now, and have been very happy for the last three months."[10] But her avowal of adjustment was accompanied by the decision to leave for Hong Kong by way of Honolulu and Japan, then on to India, and eventually England again. Although she claimed to have been "very happy for the last three months" that happiness was tempered by the memory of the preceding months in California when she believed herself to be "down and out & . . . a failure."[11] In an undated letter from that period she apologized for "Bad manners [which] were unintentional and completely unsuspected by me. . . . All this is by way of getting my conscience unloaded before retiring from active service, so to speak. It is so obviously time for me to get back to my old Living Alone, I was best like that even in England, where my 'English manners' didn't show—It was stupid of me to forget the inevitable effect of them on California."[12]

When Benson left San Francisco she left an area she was to return to and some people with whom she was forging the lasting bond of deep friendship. She took with her the beginning of a growing contempt for most things American and the memory—no, the immediate pain—of personal unhappiness.

Before ever arriving in California Benson had observed to both Harriet Monroe and Amy Lowell that "it is rather hopeless for Americans and English each to try to understand what the other is driving at" because "English and American experience has been in two different worlds for the last four years at least, and it is not to be expected that we should express ourselves in the same way, or really understand each other's ideals."[13] The American feeling that the war in Europe had been an unpleasantness quickly settled by the decisive American intervention on the side of the Allies must have been rather grating to someone who had lived through the years of European and English agony which led up to the American entry into the fray. Furthermore, Ellis Roberts claimed that Benson was seriously disturbed by what she felt to be the Americans' betrayal of their president when they declined to support Woodrow Wilson's idea for a League of Nations.[14] However, there were more fundamental differences, apparently, in personal perspective between Benson and her California friends.

Benson was twenty-seven during the year she was in California. She had already published two novels and a book of poetry before she left England, and a third novel was completed and published while she was in California. She had lived alone in London and had travelled alone to the United States; she had supported herself by working on a farm in Colorado, and in California by collecting bills, selling boys' books, giving French lessons, lecturing to an English class at the University of California, and working as a reader for the University Press. In spite of all this she did not consider herself part of the "adult world." For instance, in writing about a dinner at which she was co-hostess she claimed that it was "surprisingly *grown-up* considering that we had no help in organizing it" (italics added).[15] About the same time, she asked the American writer Witter Bynner to read the manuscript of *Living Alone*, which she said was "hardly a quarter of the size of a real *grown-up* novel" (italics added).[16] Benson seemed to feel that she was really a child presumptuous enough to pose as an adult. Augmenting her mental participation in this role, she had physical props that furthered the illusion. The novelist Ida A. Wylie met Benson while she was in California this first time and described her later as "a thin bean-pole of a girl with the gaunt wan look of a medieval page in the last stages of consumption."[17] A child entering into the game of "grown-up" and believing that those with whom she is playing are indeed "grown-up" might believe that there are some unspoken rules to which the grownups will adhere. Benson, in spite of her professed disillusion, seemed to have this childlike innocence. The activities she engaged in certainly seemed grown-up. Parties, drinking, "binges" as she called them, all night dinners, moonlight trips to the mountains, to the beaches, intense emotion of some sort—confidences and tipsy discussions—this was her grown-up world. The problem may well have been that the grown-up world into which she plunged was populated with adults acting like children. If her California friends did not have Benson's innocence, yet assumed the role of innocence, they may have been operating in a ruleless world of fear. The jaded or frightened personality which looks back nostalgically on what may be an illusory innocence and freedom of childhood brings a certain cynicism and desperation to the game of recapturing that mythic carefree life. Benson may not have noticed this qualitative difference in perception, but she felt and eventually articulated a growing antipathy for much of the California life.

Benson's distress was given focus, and indeed probably was precipitated by, an unsatisfactory romance. Whereas in England Benson had been the importuned, in California she was in competition with a friend for the attention of a man who apparently did not return her affection—or at least not as intensely and exclusively as she felt was necessary.

In January, 1920, a weary Stella Benson left San Francisco for China. By the time she reached Hong Kong in February she had dislocated her shoulder and had been so ill with influenza that the ship's captain had tried—unsuccessfully—to put her off the ship. In Hong Kong she taught young boys in a mission school, then left to work for three months as an X-ray technician at the Rockefeller Institute in Peking. In September, despite the many small wars being waged throughout China, she travelled with two friends up the Yang-tse river. In a besieged Chungking she met "one Shaemas O'Gorman Anderson, a curious and clever twinklebud with an untethered eyeglass."[18] This "twinklebud" not only extricated the marooned Benson and her friends from the dangers of Chungking, but, in spite of an existing romantic commitment, became interested in Stella Benson, and she in him. However, this tremulous romance seemed directionless, and Benson resumed her odyssey, returning to Hong Kong, then leaving for India.

During the several months spent in India, she travelled, attended teas, went tiger shooting, and also found time to begin work on her fourth novel, *The Poor Man*. In the summer of 1921, shortly after Benson's return to England, Shaemas O'Gorman Anderson arrived from China. After a brief courtship Stella Benson the writer became, on September 29, 1921, Mrs. James C. O'Gorman Anderson in private life. Anderson was on leave from the Chinese Customs Service until the following summer, so the couple began an extended honeymoon trip to California on October 30, 1921.

When the Andersons arrived in New York they had only completed one half of their journey; to traverse the continent to California they bought a car. In this car, which they named Stephanie, the Andersons proposed to drive to California in spite of what their friends considered two overwhelming reasons to reject the plan. The first objection was that neither Stella nor Shaemas had ever driven, much less owned, a car. The second was that it was November; the weather would be atrocious. The weight of these objections increases when we remember that this was at a time when well-maintained two-lane highways were a luxury, gas stations did not line what roads there were with twenty-four hour service, overnight lodging was sometimes available only in one's own car, and cars' engines were far from dependable. Unswayed by these practical considerations, the Andersons left New York in November, and finally reached California in January, 1922. They rented an apartment in Berkeley and, between visits to friends and sightseeing trips, Benson finished *The Poor Man*, a novel which, because of its biting satire of American life, cost her the friendship of some Californians. In May they returned to England, visited Shaemas's family in Ireland until October, then left for his new assignment in Mengtsz, China.

The China Years: 1922–1933

The China adventure did not begin well. Benson became ill on the voyage out and spent the first several months at the new post recuperating. Six months after arriving in Mengtsz she reported "we are happyish but very much isolated here."[19] At first glance this isolation would seem to reconcile physical and psychical reality. The self-deprecating, world-mocking writer, partially deaf, convinced of her fundamental unattractiveness, should be happy removed at last from the petty social considerations, the polite amenities she claimed to find so chafing. Unhappily, all she escaped was the possibility of finding sympathetic friends. Life in China was a ceaseless ordeal of enforced sociability with people Benson found nearly unendurable. In England were minds as quick, sensibilities as delicate, and emotions as concealed as Stella Benson's. There were people who believed their illusions gone and so could build an illusory defense against the buffets of the cold, painful, and fundamentally hostile world which confronted them as it did Stella Benson. In China there were no such minds, or none that revealed themselves to this lonely writer.

After living for several years in China she became extremely annoyed by the constant praise of the Chinese and of life in the vast wildernesses of the world, and asserted that the hermit who selects the exclusive society of a million trees, an intermittent grizzley bear, a patch of willow-weed, and a pair of chickadees, is either posing, or else is actually selecting the society of his intellectual equals. . . . We enforced hermits live among our outrageously haunted solitudes making generous allowances for fellow creatures who have surely no right to be so tolerantly excused. . . . The Chinese are one of the most prosaic people in the world and have least to teach us. . . . Alas, if circumstances oblige us to live among chickadees or Chinese bureaucrats,—may we not be frank about the thing and admit that we are bored?[20]

To overcome the isolation, she kept up a steady correspondence with friends in America and England. To Sidney Schiff (Stephen Hudson) she confessed that "All the interest and pleasure in my life comes from the letters and kind ideas of friends."[21] Unhappily letters were not sufficient, and her feelings of inadequacy could no longer be disguised with the tattered cloak of worldly contempt. The scorn she had reserved for imitation-people she directed at herself.

In China there is literally no eye at all for what I am. . . . What I have of my own is not despised so much as entirely unsuspected. None of these neighbours here know me as anything but a plain woman, a poor housekeeper, a woman who has not even had a child. . . . It is the first time in my life I have ever been thrown on my own inward resources, with nothing to read and no one to talk to— . . . the effect of this isolation is to make me ponder a great deal on myself in an entirely unproductive way—and to make me hate myself most bitterly. I see how much I have depended on outside approval and flattery all my life and how nothing I am without it.[22]

Benson did put her writing before domestic duties and seemed unable to cope with servants. The extent to which she allowed herself and her household to be dominated by the tempers and whims of these servants surprised friends who visited her. However, her childlessness was not voluntary and was, even without the contempt it generated from her neighbors, a source of pain. A rough measure of the emptiness she felt without children of her own might be found in her passionate attachment to dogs. In Benson's literary works the very rocks and sand strike human attitudes, the landscape as well as its inhabitants seems a conscious force. In her private life dogs, cars, even her illnesses had names and personalities. Benson attributed a right to life, to a respected independent existence, to all things animate and inanimate; but dogs were even provided with voices. Benson would speak for her dogs, in a dog dialect which resembled human speech and was squeaky when a puppy spoke, gruff when a grown dog conversed. She freely admitted to a passion for dogs which was far out of proportion to that of the "normal" dog lover. This passion assumes a certain poignancy when viewed against the background of her admission that pets are a substitute for children, who are a substitute for immortality.[23] If the quality of the attachment to the substitute reflected the measure of the desire for the unattainable, Stella Benson must have lived with constant suffering for her childlessness. And compounding her feelings of isolation and worthlessness was the fact that her husband, though he also complained of the neighbors, did not seem to mind them as much.

Living "exclusively among people whose highest idea of wit is a joke about being drunk and whose only outlet for intelligence is Bridge,"[24] Benson published the novel *Pipers and a Dancer* (1924) and a collection of travel articles entitled *The Little World* (1925). But writing was not protection against the contempt of her neighbors or the hostility from California aroused by her novel *The Poor Man*. Although her appreciation of the natural beauty of Mengtsz never waned, the reality of its human shortcomings was so devastating that by the time Benson left after two and one half years, her confidence in herself as a person, a wife, even a writer, was severely shaken.

The Andersons were transferred to Shanghai. Although Benson welcomed the fact of the transfer, the assignment was a disappointment. "We are both very much disappointed to get Shanghai—a place we have always dreaded going to. It is neither Asia nor Europe; just a gaudy provincial commercial town transplanted into a Chinese marsh."[25] However, her dread of living in Shanghai was mitigated to some extent by the fact that, after settling her husband in their new post, she would be leaving for California and then England.

The Stella Benson Anderson who left Shanghai for California in May, 1925, was thirty-three, "nearly always physically tired,"[26] and, because of *The Poor Man*, apprehensive about her reception in California. She felt that she was reemerging from China a new, but certainly not necessarily a better woman. She admitted "The old Stella Benson who use {*sic*} to walk the world in a constant state of excitement and defensive illusionment seems to me now . . . a remote and unknown person. . . . Various things have made me feel very far removed from friends and from my youth during these last two years."[27]

Benson revised the manuscript of a novel during the voyage to California and was enthusiastic about it by the time she arrived there. The book became one of her best, *Goodbye, Stranger*. During her brief visit to California she was pleased to discover that the outcry against *The Poor Man* had abated, so she was quite content when she saw her older brother in the Bahamas, then her family in England. In the meantime Shaemas had been reassigned, so when Benson left for China in September, 1925, her destination was not Shanghai, but Lung Ching Tsun, "on the edge of Manchuria and Siberia where one wears fur jodpores for nine months of the year and no neighbors within fifty miles."[28]

Lung Ching Tsun was even more isolated than Mengtsz: "This is not a very happy place—and I don't seem to have the courage to face either the intense cold or the loneliness very well."[29] After a year and a half she seemed resigned to an intellectual stagnation and reported, "I have, for instance, at the moment, almost no thoughts outside my new horse, Julian, whom I helped to be born on Monday. . . . I am writing nothing, and not expecting to write anything."[30] Though she read and re-read the novels of Jane Austen, newspapers, magazines, and books sent by friends, Benson was unable to continue with her own writing. She felt "extremely middleaged"[31] and devoted herself to her garden and pets, especially her dogs and puppies.

One brief, husbandless excursion to California, from December, 1926, to March, 1927, was provided for rest and revitalization. Other than that, short excursions in China and Japan were the only relief from life on a truly remote outpost. However, there were local distractions, albeit not of a particularly intellectually challenging nature.

In Lung Ching Tsun Benson's prejudices against missionaries were reinforced. Although she recognized intelligent individual missionaries, she believed such individuals atypical. She held the same general opinion of Americans, French, and Irish. However, not all of her experiences in Lung Ching Tsun were negative. It was there that another prejudice was formed, but this a positive one. "The Russians are the debris of the White Army, mostly scamps and prostitutes, but they seem all intelligent and all musical—infinitely more attractive neighbors than the missionaries."[32] She described Russians with many of the characteristics attributed to the French in Mengtsz, yet the Russians were irresistible rather than resented. "There is something very irresistible about Russians to me. . . . We are suffering rather from Russians just now. I still admire them as a race—unreasonably, I suppose—but they certainly are exasperating when they Get Busy Being like Anglo-Saxons—and so complacent (with a sort of fatalistic masochistic complacency) in their futility. 'That is the Russian Character,' they say with a look of pleased humility which makes me (when in a practical mood) want to bite them."[33] These Russians were, along with her dogs, a source of interest during the long months of exile in the wastes of Manchuria. They also proved to be a source of inspiration for her most successful novel, *Tobit Transplanted* (published in America as *The Far-away Bride*). She did not begin the novel until after she had left Lung Ching Tsun, but this retelling of the tale of Tobit from the Apocrypha with Russian rather than Jewish exiles was to become her best-known and most highly acclaimed work. In 1932 it won the Vie Heureuse Prize and the A. C. Benson (she was not related to that Benson family) silver medal "for services to literature."

After slightly more than two years in Lung Ching Tsun the Andersons took a two-year leave in Europe. This two-year holiday was not a happy one, and was punctuated for Benson by a serious illness. Finally, still weak from a bout with influenza, she sailed alone to visit her brother George in the Bahamas. There she began her new novel and rested in the sun. She returned to England in March to see her husband off for China, but she did not join him until September.

A friend described the Andersons as, "he, romantic, inclined to moods of gloom, a shade sentimental; she, realist, fanciful, pessimistic and with a diamondhard core of irresponsible gaiety."[34] The Anderson marriage continued after the catastrophic leave, but the Stella Benson who rejoined her husband in Nanning in 1929 was more firmly convinced of the essentially solitary nature of life. Communication was imperfect, and complete understanding impossible. The result of this conviction was not a cynicism but rather what appeared to be, in her writing, a compassion which softened the blows of reality. Benson had felt personally neglected; her identification would henceforth be professional. She believed that as an artist, a woman artist, she had a special contribution to make and she clung to this role. In a letter to her husband she explained the terms on which their life together would resume.

I insist on being a writer first and a wife second: a man artist would insist and I insist. . . . Apart from that, I insist that I have a right to have a married life, to be fond of you and be faithful to you, and have you fond of me and faithful (more or less) to me, as long as your feeling warrants this. . . . I wasn't *born* to be a wife to anyone, but to be a writer—However I am your wife, and I'm very glad I am: and if only you would realize that I can only be the kind of wife I am—only secondarily domestic—it would be much better . . . I . . . wish you would clear your mind of what you think a wife *ought* to be, and just think of what I am. . . . All wives are persons, really—not primarily wives; and their person-side has to be tolerated by all the persons that marry them.[35]

Times and Places 13

The six months spent in Nanning, a "hot, snakey, palmy garden," were trying but busy. Between rumors of local Chinese wars, kidnapping alarms, and actual shooting and bombing, Benson managed to finish *Tobit Transplanted*, the novel which was begun in the aftermath of the pain of 1928. Nonetheless, the absence of intellectual intercourse in Nanning, as in Mengtsz and Lung Ching Tsun, was sorely felt. Eventually, even people themselves began to appear slightly unreal.

Now that I am growing deafer and deafer, I have got into the habit of watching lips moving—chins wobbling—hands gesturing—rather than trying to hear words. And, watching in this way, it often seems to me that the real body is too busy—blowing unreality into the air, in the shape of words that have no relation to reality at all. It seems to me in these moods that we are nothing but houses—each with a ghost in the attic.

I am not sure that I am really growing deafer, but a life with neighbors who, I can always be sure, will never say anything that I really want to hear, is making me more and more inattentive as well as more amiable. I have learned to sit hour by hour just watching lips moving, and keeping my mind clear of the sound of words.[36]

Her isolation in that letter sounds almost complete, but as she was soon to learn, she still did hear what people said, and what they said still could give her pain.

The Andersons were finally rescued from Nanning in April, just before friends in England finalized plans to hire a plane to fly in and get them out of the city before it was razed by the warring Chinese armies. Their new assignment in Hong Kong was certainly much safer, had more dependable mails and a much larger community of Englishmen (and women), but unhappily Benson still could not find the company she sought. She found that conversations were still limited to bridge and gossip, and her identity as an artist was still no identity at all. Indeed, in Hong Kong, which would appear to be a place where ideas *could* be exchanged, where books, magazines, and newspapers were more or less readily available, her self-esteem was dealt a blow which could not have been administered in a remoter station.

Tobit Transplanted was quite different in style from her earlier work, and Benson was excited about its prospects. Its absence from the bookstore shelves of Hong Kong prompted an inquiry, which elicited the response that no copies of *Tobit* had been ordered because there didn't seem to be any audience for her work. In a remoter location such indifference might not have had such power to wound, but Hong Kong was supposed to be an English enclave in China, an intellectual oasis for the isolated writer. She admitted that though she was becoming outwardly callous to such slights, the pain was none the less real.[37] Nine months later she claimed at last to have become indifferent to the opinions of others, but the last sentence in her avowal reveals the source of her newly proclaimed independence, as well as the nonexistence of that independence.

I do at last truly think I have reached the stage where I am not humiliated by the contempt of the stupid; but this state was slow in being achieved. People of inferior understanding have had power until very recently to make me miserably unhappy; but now my worm-like vanity has turned at last. . . . For the first time in my life I can be despised by the majority—for *what I am*—and still not regret being what I am. . . . Here in Hongkong I am definitely despised for being what I am, that is, One of Those Clevah Women—a Nauthoress—a Woman who thinks herself the Equal of a Man, etc.—But I don't care a damn, I really do believe—now. Perhaps it is only because I have now found the few people in Hongkong who don't mind these qualities.[38]

Among the people who did not mind her qualities were those engaged in a campaign against the selling of young girls into government brothels. The young suffragette who had worked to secure insurance for English prostitutes grew into a woman crusading against sexual slavery for the sport of English seamen. In a letter to Sidney Schiff she explained, "engaged as I am in this campaign, I seem to be surrounded by people who talk about moral ought-to-be's. I don't know whether chastity is necessary or unnecessary, possible or impossible—all I know is that whatever creature *is* must be allowed to continue to *be*—and that the child sold into a brothel at fifteen years old is a human creature trespassed upon."[39] As had been the case with her earlier reforming activities, the result of this campaign was not all that she had hoped. But her efforts did focus much-needed attention upon a practice eventually to be modified officially.

Before Benson left Hong Kong in January, 1932, to visit California and England, she was glowing over the fact that "Tobit—(The Far-away Bride)—has had rather a pleasing success in that it has been chosen to represent England in the international competition got up by the P.E.N. Club—supposed to be, in the committee's opinion, the best book published in that country during the last two years."[40] When she arrived in San Francisco she spread the good news: "I am to have a medal pinned onto this chest by the Royal Society of Literature—for my 'services to Literature' in writing Tobit—and I heard last night a far far better thing—that Tobit has won the French prize (Vie Hereuse) by unanimous vote"[41] In London she found she was the acclaimed authoress, deluged with mail, besieged with invitations, and assailed with commissions for articles. The excitement and the prospect of increased financial security from her writing gave her courage. The footloose life of the traveller, of the wife of a Chinese customs agent, was tiring, and she began making plans to settle eventually with her husband into a permanent home. The permanence, however, was not of the present, and in August, 1932, she sailed for China once again.

Oppressed by her isolation and unhappy that as a woman in China she seemed to be of no importance at all, Benson wrote to Virginia Woolf that "The keynote of China, I have decided, is a *Booming*; a male voice Booming in a female ear, Booming instruction almost always incorrect, or Booming boasts."[42] The Booming might not have been so unbearable if she could have Boomed back, but unfortunately, "Only male voices are heard, in China."[43] After only two months at this new post, weak in health and isolated from congenial companions, she closed a letter to a California friend with love, then added, "if only love were more potent, how very quickly the Depression would lift. Here we are all sending love to each other all over the world—and what's the use. Though we love till we are black in the face, the world remains apparently just as loveless as before. However, here is my love, dropping into the void like the rest."[44] For Benson love, as well as more mundane forms of communion, seemed powerless against the invisible but impenetrable walls insulating each solitary individual from the understanding of his fellow men.

In China, among "people whose faces freeze the instant you say something spontaneous or homemade,"[45] with what she had already announced would be her last novel only two-thirds finished, Stella Benson O'Gorman Anderson died on December 6, 1933.

Chapter Two
The Singular Voice

From the first, Stella Benson has had loyal followers, but their numbers have not been legion. Although her books received generally favorable reviews, they were occasionally criticized for their treatment of their subject. Thus, there was too much about women's suffrage in *I Pose*, too close a brush with immorality in *This Is the End*, too unpleasant a character in *Poor Man*, and too fragmented a personality in *Pipers and a Dancer*. All reviewers recognized Benson's remarkable wit, but for some it was too much of a good thing, for others too iconoclastic. Yet acting upon a thoroughly modern inclination to question eternal verities, and treating the acute modern sense of isolation in all of her work, Benson made no radical departures from traditional literature in either technique or theme.

Strictly speaking, all of Benson's novels and most of her short stories are narrated from the first-person point of view. The voice of the narrator is strongest in her first novel, in which the unnamed narrator is as important as the two central characters, a suffragette and a gardener. The narrator offers the essential light touch to contrast with the uninterrupted seriousness of the suffragette and the unrelieved self-centeredness of the gardener. The second novel opens with a bit of special pleading from the narrator, but the personality of the narrator diminishes steadily through the rest of the novels. There is always the sense of wit and the delightful puncturing of pretension in all Benson novels, but the personality of the narrator recedes and becomes less obtrusive in her later work. The last four novels have the feel of the Victorian third-person narrations with occasional authorial intrusions, as in Thackeray's *Vanity Fair* when the narrator addresses the reader directly.

By the time Stella Benson began writing, Dorothy Richardson had already begun her twelve-volume exploration of feminine consciousness, *Pilgrimage*, and May Sinclair had already labelled Richardson's narrative technique "stream of consciousness." Before Benson was at the midpoint of her writing career, James Joyce had published *Ulysses*, perhaps the best-known example of the stream-of-consciousness technique. This narrative method allows for exhaustive exploration of the mind of one character, usually at the expense of humor and interest in varied characters. That cost was too high, and Benson remained with more traditional methods of narration, although she did incorporate to advantage elements of the new style.

Benson is able to characterize with a few deft strokes, and her riveting analysis of characters and her lightness of touch would be impossible in the self-absorption necessary for the stream-of-consciousness or interior monologue. However, Benson often achieves a similar effect through an ambiguity of perspective. For instance, in the later novel *Goodbye, Stranger*, a young woman is disconsolate because her husband of seven years has told her that he loves another woman. Being escorted back to her house by her dog Josephine and a young man who has been nursing a harmless romantic fantasy about her, Daley is genuinely distraught because she doesn't understand the attraction of the other woman, and she knows that her husband's announcement—it was not so weak as a mere admission—is to be taken seriously.

> Lion took her hand in his and they walked thus, linked together, in the light shade of the bamboos.
> Josephine fitted her nose like a cork into a mousehole. She blew down the hole, perhaps to asphyxiate the mouse, and then inhaled deeply. She wagged her tail, showing that she was confident that the mouse would be caught by this method, would swoon and be sucked by her strong upward snuffling to the mouth of the hole, as lemonade is sucked up a straw. "If only dogs knew a little more natural science. . . " thought Daley vaguely with half her mind. "But then the world would be impossible for mice."[1]

Clearly the first sentence above is the narrator's recording of fact. But the personification of the dog with her grand and impractical scheme to exhale carbon monoxide into the hole, then vacuum up the victim as a morsel to burst upon the palate with the welcome savor of refreshing lemonade—this vision of exuberant conception and joyful execution is characteristic of Daley and is in fact her view of the scene as her absentminded comment reveals. The entire scene comes to the reader as effortlessly and vividly as it does to Daley, as does her immediate sympathy for both the dog whose plan goes awry and the mouse who would be victim. This light play of the imagination upon the world around her is automatic with Daley. She gains the reader's sympathy because she is so alive to the world around her and so incapable of prolonged self-pity. But with this same image we see how Benson manages to gain a certain sympathy for the woman who has caused Daley so much unhappiness. Delightful as the vision of the dog's mind is, it is not the sort of thing that should intrude upon the grief of a character in romantic decline. Thus, in one stroke and with no explicit comment Benson offers the reader a delightful image, reveals the responsiveness of Daley to the life around her, and gently suggests Daley's resilience in unhappiness. Benson uses to advantage what she needs of stream of consciousness while maintaining a traditional approach to the novel.

Benson laces several of her novels with strong doses of fantasy; but in this practice she was not alone. She lived in an age wracked by insecurity, and a rather common method of coping has always been to close one's eyes to the reality around one. In 1904 Peter Pan flew into the life of England, and his triumph became even more firmly rooted after the war. J. M. Barrie's creation who refused to grow up had a whole nation of well-wishers. Walter de la Mare, a writer Benson read with great pleasure, also dealt with the world just beyond practical knowledge. Although his short stories have fallen from favor, his poems, especially the mysterious "Listeners," are still often anthologized, and G. K. Chesterton's whimsy still finds an audience. But this resort to fantasy was not confined to men. After Benson was moving away from fantasy in her own work, Virginia Woolf's *Orlando* offered its public an androgynous being who, over the course of several centuries, had both male and female form. The determination not to be held to an external reality was characteristic of the first quarter of the twentieth century; Benson's inclusion of fantasy in her novels was not unique.

The fantasy accompanies an apparent dismay at the world, but the dismay is no sure sign of despair. It is not at all uncommon for writers whose works do not seem overtly optimistic to be accused of being at least pessimistic, at times even nihilistic. In 1923 Benson listed Thomas Hardy with Joseph Conrad and D. H. Lawrence as the three greatest living writers. Yet, about the time of Benson's birth, Hardy had given up writing novels altogether following the outcry against the pessimism of *Jude the Obscure*. Joseph Conrad's work, while upholding romantic values, seems to admit that they are helpless against the world. The dark visions of Hardy and Conrad made their way into the novels of Stella Benson. The difference is that whereas Hardy and Conrad could present worlds laden with foreboding and ominous with meaning, Benson presents a gray world whose desolation is lightened by a determined wit asserting itself against defeat. The light touch averting tragedy contrasts sharply with the works of others who also confronted a world in which welcoming nature seemed absent. For the 1920s T. S. Eliot's *The Waste*

Land chronicled the disassociation of humanity in the unreal city of the world. Later, in the 1930s, W. H. Auden explored desolate landscapes over which mysterious and inevitable antagonisms strained. Neither man admitted to or finally demonstrated a conviction that evil or even purposelessness dominated the world, although both recognized loneliness (Eliot) and alienation (Auden) as characteristic of the human condition of the time. Benson shared their recognition and offered as armament irony, understatement, and arresting visual images.

In an explicitly feminist novel Benson often achieves her point not through lecturing but through irony. A description of women in deck chairs on an ocean voyage reveals the emptiness and banality of their lives while suggesting their repressed frustration. "The silence of the unintroduced at first lay, like a pall, along the deck-chairs, but a mutual friend was quickly found in Mothersill, whose excellent invention was represented in every work-bag. The bright noise of women discussing suffering rippled along the garden. Abuse of the *Caribbeania's* stewardesses sprang from lip to lip. It was a pretty scene."[2] The irony of the contemplation of suffering as a pleasure-producing occupation, the conclusion that this was a pretty scene, draws the reader toward criticism of the conventional woman's world.

Irony may become supercilious and cloying if it is the exclusive vehicle of the agile mind. Benson was well aware of this fact and moderated the flip tone with effective understatement. For example, an account of the aftermath of an earthquake demonstrates Benson's descriptive restraint in the face of crisis.

The High Street looked as if one side of it had charged the other with equally disastrous results to both. At different points in it, fire and heavy smoke were animating the scene. Distracted men and women panted and moaned and tore at the wreckage with bleeding hands. A little crying crowd was collected round a woman who lay nailed to the ground by a mountain of brick with her face fixed in a glare of terrible surprise. By the cathedral steps the dead lay in a row, shoulder to shoulder, with the horrid uniformity of sprats upon a plate.[3]

Rather than trying to convey the enormity of the horror through realistic, lurid detail, Benson's description seems to emphasize what is not said. The first sentence establishes an air of unreality by suggesting a child's game. Inanimate objects cannot themselves move; what could explain this improbable destruction? The second sentence begins the horror as fire and smoke visually liven the still rubble while the reader knows they will increase the number of dead. Beginning the next sentence, *distracted*, with its meaning of "absent-minded" as well as "desperately confused," maintains a low-key tone for the description as a more forceful word—*frantic* or *desperate*—would not. No word is necessary, of course, to explain why the people tore at the wreckage. The next sentence emphasizes the number of people grieving rather than the single dead woman, and finally, "the horrid uniformity of sprats upon a plate" gives a peculiarly pedestrian image to the particularly horrible fact. The effect is to distance the reader from the fact of death thus reducing the reader's resistance to the idea of unromantic, inevitable death.

Complementing Benson's quiet undercutting of the awful and the grand is her vivid focus on the common occurrence that operates to exalt the world and the life within it. And after all, the omnipresence and variety of life are at the heart of all of her work. There may be a gray pall over the world of some of Benson's novels, but that is a background across which flash brilliant images of life and light. These images which linger in the mind are not simple adornment. They contribute to the mood and theme of the work. For instance, two young men, indifferent to the landscape, are walking through Korea:

Seryozha and Wilfred Chew began their journey in a happy sunlight swimming with swallows. Neither Seryozha nor Wilfred saw the birds. And indeed, birds are transparent, I think, like the safe anonymous shapes of sheep on hillsides or policemen at city crossings; these things are part of fitness, they are so native to the air that they become glass to the attention.
. . .
Koreans in Kanto are worn by custom to the same fine transparency as birds and other lovely and common furnishings of the scene; they are to the eye what the gentle ticking of a clock is to the ear. Yet today, since it was a Korean holiday, the Korean wanderers were so gaily dressed as to catch even an accustomed eye. Favourite colours were arsenic green, poison pink, apple green and a cheap crude blue—all very unflowerlike colours, yet they sowed the roads and fields and paths with an effect of flowers.[4]

In the first part of the quotation Benson develops the feeling of luxuriant life while in the second she produces a friendly acceptance of the exotic. With the word *swimming* Benson suggests not just reeling flocks of birds but also teeming schools of fish which are no doubt present though not visible in the distant river that is "broad, polished and set in a pale bed thinly shaded with pink-osiers." The comparison of the birds to quiet sheep or protective policemen brings comfort and safety to this exotic setting and leads the reader to a calm acceptance of the universality of beauty. Next the exotic people are aligned with things ordinary—

birds, sheep, policemen, and ticking clocks—before being cast in the stark glare of strangeness. Arsenic green and poison pink? A description of a choice of colors that our enemies might make: those sadly lacking in the perfect taste or relaxed sense of color that we admit to our own wardrobes. But the venom is withdrawn with the admission that, taken all together, there is everywhere "an effect of flowers."

The pure enjoyment of the scene is readily apparent even from these brief quotations. The multiplicity of colors, shapes, comparisons, and settings compressed within a description of a countryside is characteristic of the vision of the girl toward whom the two young men are travelling, This girl will give up her own sense of transparency by drawing a flying swallow above her name on a marriage contract. Thus the description gives the reader an idea of the actual land through which two young men are walking; it develops the idea of teeming, colorful life as entertainment for the eyes; and it introduces an idea of the transparency that a young girl imagines for herself as she seeks to avoid commitment to a husband. An effective symbol must first be whatever it literally is in an artistic work. Benson's development of symbols is unobtrusive, her images highly effective because they are always appropriate, fresh, and unclichéd.

Stella Benson's work is much more than a compilation of irony, understatement, and vivid images. She uses these techniques to convey the emotional detachment and visual involvement of characters who feel estranged from, but have a deep appreciation for, life. Like Charles Dickens she can capture a type in a few quick strokes; like Evelyn Waugh she can spot the emptiness behind the facade, but she rejects both the melodrama and broad social satire of these writers. Benson's recurring concern is the isolation of the individual in the modern world. And her vision is broad enough, her compassion great enough, to include both sexes in her sympathy.

Compassionate toward the plight of individuals, Benson's work does not take on the anti-masculine bias found in the work of some feminists. It does, however, focus on the situation of women in society. There is from first to last the recognition that society expects women to be content with women's place, which is in the home. Benson's heroines, by chance or by choice, are not in their place. With two possible exceptions her novels do not chronicle a love affair. Even more significantly not only do the heroines not fall in love, they consciously reject potential lovers and husbands. The character who comes closest to believing herself in love commits suicide rather than lock herself into the prison that marriage would be. In one of the two novels ending with a marriage the heroine accepts marriage as a defeat of all that is private and personal in herself. No more than two or three sentences in the entire novel are devoted to the young man involved, and they explain that he has already been rejected once. He is given no negative traits; he is simply not important. Although never considered particularly desirable by her heroines, the men in Benson's novels are not portrayed more harshly than the women.

Developing interest in the emotional life of women has increasingly been translated into ever more explicit discussion of their sex lives. Stella Benson does not offer extended musings on matters explicitly sexual. Her work explores the profound effect of women's discomfort with their place in society as they reject, ignore, or fear their feminine roles. The absence of explicit sex is not a sign of literary repression but the recognition that a woman's discontent with her political and social position must of necessity affect the way she sees herself in every way, including as a sexual creature. Although the novels recognize that as far as the world is concerned a woman's identity is established by her relationship with men, the women in Benson's novels attempt to ignore that standard. The attempt of ordinary women to define themselves is the subject of the novels. These women are neither unusually attractive nor especially talented. But what is indeed remarkable about them is that they do not find their own significance in their emotional relationships. If they have a strong sense of personal identity, they seek to avoid personal entanglement with the outside world; if they welcome involvement with other people, they are seen wrestling with a fragmented perception of personal identity.

Unlike May Sinclair, or much later, Iris Murdoch, Benson does not assert particular intellectual positions. Nor does she try for the shimmering flow of Virginia Woolf. Offering enchanting images of the world around her, Benson conveyed the singular world within. Finally unable to envision an acceptable alternative to accepting woman's place, she came to an emphasis on the recognition of "otherness," an emphasis similar to D. H. Lawrence's. In her last finished novel, *Tobit Transplanted*, the fact that a couple can recognize the essential isolation and personal vulnerability of their situation is the token of their compatibility and potential happiness.

In addition to novels Stella Benson also wrote short stories, articles for newspapers and magazines, and poetry. Oddly enough, her short stories often just miss success while her articles are excellent. Her poetry, much of which was incorporated as chapter introductions in her novels, has a lyric beauty as it cries out against despair.

Benson's recurring subject is the isolation of modern man, but it was never her intention to suggest that all is futile. Perhaps her position is made most clear in a letter she wrote trying to explain why she so strongly disliked Aldous Huxley's *Those Barren Leaves*.

Surely a book that no-one could believe and continue to live, is—if it has significance, wicked,—if it has none, worthless. It isn't a matter of being honest, of stripping the veil from a sham, it is a matter of pretending to catch truth out, of showing up life as a sham, of being waggish at the expense of truth. It is true that all the moralities and the standards have crumbled away—it is quite easy and indeed inevitable now to tear away all the coverings of words and certainties and standards in which man has wrapped himself away. Everything can be proved to be a sham—everything can and should be made a fool of— except life itself. But life itself *isn't* a butt for ingenious young men— — —life *is* worth living— — — . . . I don't believe . . . that goodness and badness exist or that nobility is anything more fundamental than opportunity or that conduct can be defined according to any standard other than taste—but I do think that genuine human feeling, reality of emotion, individuality . . . are all that we have, all that is left to us now to respect, the nearest thing we have to something sacred.[5]

Chapter Three
Public Facade and Private Identity

Stella Benson's first novel, *I Pose*, appeared in England in 1915 and in the United States the next year. In both countries women's rights were issues that, whatever one might have felt about them, one could not ignore. Nor can the subject be ignored in this novel. One of the two main characters is identified simply as "the Suffragette" (the other is simply "the Gardener"), and though only one episode is devoted to overt political activity (a women's march in London), the suffragette *does* repeatedly threaten to blow up property in protest for women's rights. However, the essential question in the novel is not, What can be done to improve society? The essential question is explicitly articulated in the final lines of the novel as the narrator confronts the problem of establishing identity: "Yes, I pose of course. But the question is—how deep may a pose extend?" As the smoke of the final explosion clears, the concerns of the narrator rise as the haunting question of identity and individual significance in an imperfect world.

The "I" of the title is the unnamed narrator of the story, and the two main characters are identified only as a gardener and a suffragette. The gardener is "not lively: but he lived, and that at least is a great merit." He is a "blue man, born to the sea," whose "chief characteristic was a whole heart in all that he did."[1] What he does is assume and discard a continuous parade of poses. While posing as a wanderer he meets a very plain-looking militant suffragette carrying a mustard-colored portmanteau with the contents of which she intends to blow up houses for the sake of votes for women. They have a brief conversation, then part, but accidentally meet again the next day. At this second meeting the gardener is struck by both the personal frailty and the potential destructiveness of the suffragette. Catching her by the arm as she attempts to leave him, he asks her to accompany him on a voyage to the Trinity Islands. She consents.

Among the passengers travelling on the ship *Caribbeania* to the Trinity Islands are Courtesy, a fat, red-haired, and very practical young woman; Mrs. Rust, whose hair is "dyed a forcible crimson"; Mrs. Rust's maid, Elizabeth Hammer, who is dying painfully of cancer; and Father Christopher, an Anglican priest who soon reveals himself as a soulless, narrow-minded horror.

At the first stop the suffragette attempts to leave the gardener and the ship. He finds her, forces from her the admission that this attempted flight is, like her earlier futile attempts to rescue the doomed Elizabeth Hammer who had thrown herself over the side of the ship, prompted by hysteria. In the first instance the suffragette was unable to allow a fellow human being to perish unaided, so she risked her life for a comparative stranger. In the second instance, the flight from the gardener, the hysteria was caused by the fear of the emotional bond being formed between them. The suffragette and the gardener return to the ship together, but their reunion is short-lived. As soon as the ship docks again, the suffragette disappears. Before the gardener finds her, the town (Union Town) suffers an earthquake. In the meantime the suffragette finds her way to Greyville, where she becomes nurse-companion to a rather unpleasant, pretentious, ill young boy named Albert. When the gardener finally discovers the suffragette, Albert's health has worsened, and Albert, his aunt Miss Brown, and the suffragette leave for England.

Albert dies during the voyage, so when the ship reaches England the suffragette returns to her role of worker in the suffrage movement. Her efforts to convince working girls to demand at least subsistence wages are thwarted by Father Christopher, in whose parish she is working. (This is the same priest who was travelling on the *Caribbeania*.) When she learns that the gardener has also returned to England and is looking for her, she decides to see him. Their meeting concludes with her suggestion that they marry the following Tuesday. At this point the first chapter, 302 pages long, ends where the book should end if it is to have the traditional happy ending in which convention wins both the characters and the reader to approval of its merits. As E. M. Forster has observed, "Any strong emotion brings with it the illusion of permanence, and the novelists have seized upon this. They usually end their books with marriage, and we do not object because we lend them our dreams."[2] The conventional thing for the suffragette to do is to settle down in marriage with the gardener. The prospect of the suffragette's marriage and her implied abandonment of the women's suffrage movement strongly reinforce the idea that the woman's place *is* in the home. It would seem that the suffragette has finally realized that only in a home of her own with a husband to care for will she be happy. The myth that domesticity will bring contentment has certainly been encouraged in Western society. But Stella Benson's novels do not deal with dreams encouraging easy acquiescence in conventional values.

In the eight pages of the final chapter the hypocrisy and evil of Father Christopher are incontrovertibly established, and the gardener's pleased preparation for his marriage and his even-tempered disregard for the suffragette's telegram telling him not to go to their meeting place are recorded. He goes anyway, and finds the suffragette there with her mustard-colored portmanteau. They eat together, leave together, and the reader and the gardener expect a wedding to occur. Instead, when they pause at a church, the suffragette approaches the altar, hurls the portmanteau, and blows up herself and the chancel screen.

I Pose, witty and indignant, is entertaining while offering criticism of the social and political order of its time. Organized causes, commercialized art, and institutionalized religion are castigated because they evince a failure of belief and an absence of commitment to a moral purpose. However, one of Benson's strengths is her ability to remind us that "they" are people. The suffrage movement is a movement of individual men and women; not all are selflessly devoted to the cause. Organized charity requires the efforts of individuals to carry out charitable missions; individual charity workers overlook the emotional needs of the recipients of charity. Finally, God's stewards in the world are after all human: an individual priest whose prayers are empty formulas, whose parishioners are expected to accept their secular lot and not try to improve it, whose bad advice to a well-intentioned man causes a worthy young girl to despair, is not the best recommendation for organized religion.

The novel is most obviously concerned with the problem of women's place in society, yet it is neither a panegyric to the nobility of women nor a diatribe against the depravity of men. Two of the three most devastating portraits in the novel are of women. In a book that advocates women's rights, the Chief Militant Suffragette, the leader of this organized cause, is mercilessly revealed in her limited commitment to that cause. Further, a novelist who might be able to affect the values of her audience is shallow and egotistical. Finally, however, the most contemptible character in the novel is a man: Father Christopher, the religious head of the Brown Borough.

Although most individuals working for reform may be sincere and committed, there is little hope expressed in the novel that effective change will ever occur. One of the participants in a women's march is a young woman carrying a baby.

> "Wiv Parliament, for instance," said the little mother . . . "They seits an' argoos about Welsh Establishment, an' all the while I 'ed my little gel die of underfeeding, becos I wuz carryin' this one, and couldn't get work." (*IP*, 241)

Arguably, a body for national government cannot concern itself with individual cases of need, especially when the needy are so many. Nevertheless, a baby girl died because her mother was pregnant and therefore could not find work; meanwhile, the governing body was concerning itself with more important things. The situation should give one pause. But the problem is not simply a political one.

Laws are, after all, made and administered by individuals. This same young woman, disdaining more meetings and organizations, clarifies the problem of collective individual indifference:

> When my little gel died, lars' October, an' 'ole lot of lidies made enquiries, an' got me a few 'alfpence a week to get on wiv till I could get back to the box-miking. I useter 'ave to go to an orfice an' answer questions, an' the lidy useter sy she was sorry to seem 'quisitive, but she ses—If some on yer cheat, you mus' all on yer suffer. . . . Bless you, I didn' mind answering questions, but I was very low then, an' I useter tike it 'ard that none o' them lidies never seemed interested. Nobody never as't wot was the nime o' my little gel that died, nor 'ow old she was, nor nothink about her pretty wys that she useter 'have. . . . 'tisn't that they ain't kind, but it's being treated in a crowd-like as come 'ard, an' there's many feels the sime. . . . (*IP*, 245)

Charity workers are content to distribute material goods for the preservation of physical life. They are unwilling to expend the time or effort to nurture emotional life and encourage a sense of individual significance. There is no suggestion that the physical life is unimportant, simply a reminder that there can be more. Of course, the pathos of the grieving young mother surrounded by emotional indifference is compounded by the unstated but obvious observation that if she had received this financial attention before her child died, the child would still be alive. Apparently, reason dictates that need must be proved, even if the conclusive proof is the loss of a human life.

Not content with showing us Parliament busy debating and charity workers busy administering, Benson skewers the Chief Militant Suffragette. This daring married woman who cut her hair short is dedicated enough to the cause of women's rights to demand great sacrifices from others and is brave enough to attend a suffrage march secure in the knowledge that a solicitious husband will whisk her away when danger threatens.

The Chief Militant Suffragette, who believed that she held feminism in the hollow of her hand, was a born leader of women. She was familiar with the knack of wringing sacrifices from other people. She was a little lady in a minor key, pale and plaintive, with short hair, like spun sand. She dressed as nearly as possible like a man, and affected an eyeglass. She probably thought that in doing this she sacrificed enough for the cause of women. She had safely found a husband before she cut her hair. I suppose she had sent more women to prison than any one magistrate in London, but she had never been to prison herself. (*IP*, 236)

 The Chief Militant Suffragette is not committed enough to her pose to let it become her reality. Safe herself from the loneliness and physical danger faced by the women she orders about, she is less a suffragette than a woman with an interesting hobby. She risks nothing yet will not hesitate to take credit for the work that others have accomplished.
 If secular organizations, those concerned with the practical day-by-day activities of living, are not willing or able to recognize need or worth in individuals, might individuals find spiritual comfort and encouragement from aesthetic pursuits? Might the artist, the novelist, cry out against injustice or encourage self-assertion? Maybe. The narrator of *I Pose* is certainly attempting to delight and instruct, but there is a vigorous warning against commercial "art." A devastating portrait of sterility, again of a woman, is of a novelist.

She was the sort of person whose bosom enters a room first, closely followed by her chin. Black eyes and a hooked Spanish nose led the rear not unworthily. She intended to be looked at, and she hoped to be recognized as a notorious novelist. For she was a momentary novelist with a contempt for yesterday and no concern at all for tomorrow. A public of a hundred thousand housemaids was all she asked. . . . Every experience in her eyes formed a part of a printed page, surrounded by a halo of favorable reviews. She never wrote a letter without an eye on her posthumous biography, never met a notable individual without taking a mental note for the benefit of a future series of "Jottings about my Generation." Both she and the suffragette kept diaries, but only the suffragette's had a lock and key. (*IP*, 155–56, 159)

Like the Chief Suffragette, the novelist has no higher purpose than shallow self-aggrandizement. Both the secular and aesthetic leaders are inadequate to the task of improving the world because they lack a belief in and commitment to a high moral purpose. What of the spiritual leaders?

Father Christopher, representative of the Anglican church, becomes the focal point for the reader's as well as the suffragette's rage. This man whose real god is "professional duty," for whom "word-pity was the chief part of his stock in trade," abandons even professional duty when confronted by unpleasantness, finds his shallow puddle of word-pity dried up whenever confronted by anyone probing the merit of a narrow, conventional "right."

Early in the novel the priest approaches the gardener, who is standing at the rail of the *Caribbeania*, and asks what he is thinking about. The gardener replies:

"Ghosts of my enormous past, I suppose. There was a very white beach that I saw just now, with opal-coloured waves running along it, and a mist whitening the sky. There were very broad red men in grey wolf-skins, standing in the water, dragging dead bodies from the sea. There were little children, blue and thin, lying dead upon the beach. I have never seen a dead child, except those. . . ."

"You ought to write fiction, yerce, yerce," said the priest. "You have a very strong imagination."

"I have," admitted the gardener. "But not strong enough to control these visions that besiege me."

The priest, who had preached more and known less about visions than anyone I can think of, was constrained to silence. (*IP*, 58)

The narrator explains that the priest's discomfort is caused by his lack of vision; he is uncomfortable in the presence of someone whose visions are real to him. But the reader may notice that Father Christopher not only is constrained to silence when in the presence of a man with vision, the priest actually recoils from the content of the vision. At the mention of a dead child he interrupts the gardener. Death is appropriate for fiction, not for two men standing on an ocean liner. The priest moves away from an imaginative and intellectual contemplation of death with the gardener just as later he will try to escape a physical and spiritual confrontation with pain and death in the person of Elizabeth Hammer.

Soon after the aborted discussion with the gardener, the priest tries unsuccessfully to run away from Mrs. Rust's maid. Dying of cancer, Elizabeth Hammer cries "Save me, save me!" Telling him she has prayed but the pain has gotten worse, she asks Father Christopher why God has not helped her. He responds, "It is, alas, woman's part to suffer in this world" (*IP*, 82). Then, just as the gardener once grabbed the arm of the suffragette, so the priest grabs the arm of the suffering woman. The use of force is the same; the effect is the same—compliance, but the objective is different. The gardener had wanted the suffragette to accompany him on a sea voyage so that English property would be safe and because he felt protective toward the suffragette in her involuntary, feminine frailty. The priest, on the other hand, uses force not to draw the woman closer, not to help a suffering soul, but to quiet the screams of a distasteful creature who might damage his vanity. When she asks for a promise that their prayers will make her better by the morning, Father Christopher assents "not out of his faith, but because that seemed the only way to put an end to the scene. And when he prayed, in a musical clerical voice, he prayed not out of his heart, but out of his sense of what was fitting" (*IP*, 83). His hypocritical self-serving pose after the distraught woman's suicide, his bland assertion that he believes that he did comfort her, reveals him a conscious liar.

Father Christopher's inability to help the dying is matched by his disinclination to aid the living. He is a man unsuited in every way for the responsibility he holds. We have ample evidence of his failure as a spiritual counselor; through his treatment of a young girl in his parish we see that he rejects the notion of substantial improvement in material well-being for the women of his flock. Because after working hard for three years Jane Wigsky is still not paid enough to live on, she quits a job Father Christopher had secured for her. She is a hard worker, sincere in her desire to improve herself, and soon finds a man willing to employ her in a job that would improve her income, her skills, and her self-respect. She innocently gives the name of Father Christopher as a reference. Father Christopher, angered because she quit the job he found for her three years earlier, convinces her future employer that she is undependable and will be unable to handle any responsibility, then persuades him to hire a young man (of Father Christopher's choosing) instead. The result is that Jane Wigsky, unemployed and with no prospects for economic advancement, elopes. This the priest offers as proof of her immorality. The fact that the elopement was an act of desperation occurring *after* he had caused her to lose her job and *after* she realized that she would be unable, with him working against her, to find one which would support her was, to his mind, irrelevant. Jane Wigsky reported to the suffragette his reaction when she asked him if *he* could live on the wage he thought suitable for women:

'E ses as 'ow God 'ad called us to this stite of life, an' it was wicked to try an' alter it. 'E ses as women are pide what they're worth, an' God mide rich an' poor an' men an' women, an' never meant the poor to be rich, or women to be pretending they was as good as men. . . . (*IP*, 282)

Receiving favorable reviews, *I Pose* was admired for its vitality and humor and forgiven for its apparent fault—a tendency toward didacticism. For example, the reviewer in the *Nation* assessed it as an "exuberant and at times witty, but too often merely sprightly, extravaganza of unreal life . . . the author assures the reader, in a parenthesis 'You need not be afraid, there is not going to be so very much about the Cause in this book.' . . . Perhaps this is where the main pose comes in, for a very large part of the book is about 'the cause.' We guess that this is really accident—that the writer set out to be merely extravagant and amusing, and dropped into a habit."[3] Clearly there is a cause afoot in the world of the story, but the most obvious "cause," the women's suffrage movement, is neither the only nor the most important cause in the novel. *I Pose* forces the reader to consider the fundamental problems of personal identity and individual importance in a world that seldom peers behind facades. The suffragette and the underfed baby girl die because their personal identities seem to count for nothing. The baby was only important to the world as proof that its mother needed help. The suffragette was important to other people as the instrument for accomplishing their desires. She was a potential wife for the gardener, a nurse for the sick child Albert, and a worker for the Chief Militant Suffragette.

During her first meeting with the gardener, the suffragette tries to make him understand why she is what she is. "One is born a woman. . . . A woman in her sphere—which is the home. One starts by thinking of one's dolls, later one thinks about one's looks, and later still about one's clothes. But nobody marries one. And then one finds that one's sphere—which is the home—has been a prison all along" (*IP*, 13). When she found she was not safely ensconced in woman's sphere, the home, the suffragette decided to demand "the privilege of having interests as wide as the world if you like, and of thinking to some purpose about England's affairs" (*IP*, 14). Her dedication to the attainment of that goal seemed to require that she eliminate all other interests. However, she is not an emotionless automaton as is evidenced by her response to the gardener's urging that she join him on the voyage to the Trinity Islands. After feeling his hand on her arm, after hearing him say "I love the shape of your face," she realizes that she is not only "a world's worker, a wronged unit seeking rights, a coheritor of the splendour of the earth, a challenger, a warrior. . . . She discovered a fact the existence of which she had seldom, even in weak moments, suspected. She found that—taken off her guard—she was a young woman of six-and-twenty" (*IP*, 35). The suffragette is a woman, and she responds to the attentions of a man; but she is also a suffragette, a world's worker, a fanatic, and she believes that a fanatic has no time for love. In this opinion she may well be correct. As a wife she would no doubt assume the role for which she had been trained. She would become passive and submissive, or at least would try to be so. Only with her husband's consent and cooperation could she work for the cause.

The suffragette persists in identifying herself as a fanatic even though the reader perceives beneath the clenched-fist exterior the same involuntary frailty that attracted the gardener. But the gardener fails to realize what the reader might also overlook without the narrator's warning: "Constitutionally she [the suffragette] was unable to be politely firm. She must either be militant or acquiescent; she knew not the half measures of civilization" (*IP*, 163). The suffragette must be what she makes herself or be entirely the creation of another. Although the cause to which she has dedicated herself does not meet with society's approval, the role she assumes—selfless worker for the good of others—is, of course, quite consistent with the prevailing stereotype of a woman's character: modest and retiring and quiet. She must, through an act of will and aided by her bag of explosives, assert herself; without constant militancy she becomes completely submissive. When the gardener assures her that he can imagine her greeting him every morning, holding their baby, sitting before the fire, what he sees is the woman as he would have her be, as indeed she could become. But the woman before the fire would be his creation, would be assuming the pose he selects for her, not the pose of her own choosing. The role of wife would be conventionally appropriate, but would be the role that she had discovered "is a prison all along."

The life of women without men in *I Pose* is far from idyllic. In a world in which a woman's sphere is the home, a woman's identity seems dependent upon her association with men. If she is not a wife she may be identified by her association with a brother (Father Christopher's nameless sister works tirelessly, under his supervision, in his parish), a nephew (Miss Brown's duty in life seems to be to care for the sickly child Albert), or a brutal boyfriend (a woman beaten by a drunken lout says nothing against him for fear he might leave her). Even Courtesy has been sent in search of a husband by her father. Capable and organized, she responds sympathetically and effectively whenever she believes someone is in need of help. She drives tragedy from the gardener's life by fixing his broken shoelace, and, ignoring the suffragette's apparently irregular marital status, Courtesy befriends and comforts her after her ill-fated attempt to rescue the doomed Elizabeth Hammer. Recognizing Mrs. Rust's feeling of purposelessness and loneliness as she drifts on the indifferent sea with no male conspicuously her own, Courtesy accepts the position of companion and assumes husbandly control of Mrs. Rust's life. Yet when a shy and ineffectual man offers Courtesy the position for which her whole life has been a preparation, she unhesitatingly renounces the sort of independence she has with Mrs. Rust and accepts his proposal of marriage.

Shy, ill, drunk, hypocritical, or immature, the men in the novel seem weak pillars indeed to support the world of women. The gardener is likable, or would be if he were about fourteen. His infatuation for the suffragette is her first, and in all likelihood would be her only, opportunity to secure the position of wife, to find identity and occupation through submission to male dominance. Marriage to the gardener would produce the standard "happy ending" for the reader who refuses to speculate about what life would be after the closing of the book. However, the life of the wife of the gardener would be certain to be far from easy. A soft touch who is unable to manage his own finances, an impractical man of no apparent skill (it is a poor recommendation for a gardener that his only plant, a nasturtium, dies), a romantic who never considers seriously the person that the suffragette is (in spite of the fact that she is undistinguished in appearance, he affectionately asserts that anyone seeing her would notice her instantly), his first act upon meeting her is to thwart her plans by imposing his judgment, and his determination to make her his wife would thwart any possibility of her being her own woman. The gardener, younger than the suffragette and uncommitted to any single ideal, is ill equipped to protect anyone from the vicissitudes of life. Yet, if he were to marry the suffragette, it is his vision of her before a fire caring for their children that both of them accept as the future reality. Younger, less introspective, more selfish, less experienced, and more romantic than the suffragette, the gardener will dominate. The suffragette's physical suicide is more dramatic than the emotional and intellectual suicide of marriage, but perhaps no more final.

Determined to be herself, the suffragette tries to stifle sentimentality and the urge to romance. There is no sentimentality in her practical care of the sick child Albert, no romance in her work against poverty and oppression in the Brown Borough, yet there is ample evidence of love. The suffragette identity she has assumed, and to which she determinedly clings, may be less a manifestation of the essential nature of the person than a pose assumed to defend herself against the world's unkindness to the unwanted. Her spontaneous willingness to sacrifice her time, energy, and even life for anyone in need of assistance provides overwhelming evidence that her dedication to a cause is not the result of a love for humanity in general by one who dislikes people as individuals.

The character of the suffragette contains the contradiction that determined individualists face when operating in a world of cause and effect. If the suffragette is a suffragette by a choice circumscribed by the social fact that her choices were limited (she could have been simply a spinster, or a governess perhaps, but not, until she met the gardener, a wife), is the self that she chooses any less her true self because the number of roles available to her was limited? *I Pose* seems to assert, like Oscar Wilde, that the pose becomes the reality. A pose maintained establishes individual identity. But the novel also reveals the pitfalls that await those who attempt to give an exclusive focus to their lives, who believe that they can embrace only one role and that any admission of other characteristics is detrimental to the preservation of individual identity. The suffragette attempts to maintain her identity as suffragette by denying her basic identity as woman. When finally confronted with the acceptance of a facet of her person that she has tried to ignore, she is unable to reconcile what she perceives to be conflicting roles.

About the time of the publication of this novel, William Butler Yeats recognized in his well-known poem "Easter 1916" that the unchanging fanatics, the stones in the changing stream of life, may appear ridiculous to those of us who are more "reasonable," but their stony determination does transform the world around them. The Irish martyrs he celebrated did not, through their deaths, bring about a new and perfect order, but they did create a terrible beauty, they did force others to pause and consider a cause for which men and women were willing to die. The suffragette, also dedicated to a cause, reconciles the conflict between her desire to be a world's worker and the temptation to accept the passive role of wife by choosing physical death rather than risk her independent identity.

The gardener faces no such conflict. He always dedicates himself completely to the role he has assumed for the moment. The fact that he changes roles as easily and almost as often as the lungs exchange air in no way undermines his wholehearted commitment at any given moment to any given role. The gardener, with the whole range of his imagination as mine for the ore of his reality, would seem to be quite justified when he announces "I believe in myself. I believe I can do exactly what I like" (*IP*, 99). The fact that fulfilling his own desires may involve overriding the desires of others does not seem to occur to him, or to affect his theory about the power of the mind. He does seem to be living proof that the imagination moves mountains, but his success is only possible because his imagination is not wholeheartedly committed to a single purpose. As long as the gardener is willing to change direction he can give himself wholly and meet with repeated success. He attains his objectives because the unattainable objectives are discarded. Even his pursuit of the suffragette, though he realizes how necessary she is to him, is slowed by his assumption of "the melancholy pose of the Rejected One" (*IP*, 208). But it is important to recognize that the gardener's poses are not facades of hypocrisy but temporary commitments to a particular vision of himself. The poses are sincere: "Even on his deathbed the gardener will pose as a dying man" (*IP*, 121). His consciously displayed exterior coincides with his perception of his inner reality of the moment. Whereas the suffragette worked with single-minded purpose to maintain her initially chosen identity, the gardener is willing to change with a passing mood. But happiness eludes him also.

In this first novel Benson uses a carefully developed color pattern to emphasize the irremediable isolation of a woman who chooses to think and act beyond the confines of woman's sphere in society. The four dominant colors in the novel are red, blue, gray, and yellow. Red is associated with all the activity of living and dying; blue and gray, associated with the gardener and the suffragette respectively, seem to represent different manifestations of introspective personalities; and yellow becomes the emblem of both destruction and emptiness.

Red is the color that dominates the book, but it dominates by framing, not by forming the heart of the story. For the gardener, "auburn, with orange lights in the sunlight, was the colour of heat, the colour of life and love" (*IP*, 10). The girl Courtesy, with flaming hair and crimson cheeks, "suffered from all the faults that you and I—poetic souls—cannot love. She was greedy. She was fat. She could not even lose a race without suspecting the timekeeper of corruption. All the same there was something so entirely healthy and human about her, that nobody had ever pointed out to her her lack of poetry, and of the more subtle virtues" (*IP*, 77). Courtesy "was not the girl to do what was conventionally impossible," but "without ever trying to be sensational, was often unexpected by mistake" (*IP*, 68, 138). She could stifle her curiosity about what she believed to be scandalous out of consideration for another person's privacy, and she could countermand the wishes of Father Christopher, who wished to gather only the "gentler and worthier" victims of the Union Town earthquake, with a spontaneous,

"Rot, . . . What do his morals matter when he's broken his leg?" (*IP*, 92). Although Courtesy embodies all the petty tyrannies which can dominate the life of convention, she also exemplifies the reality of vibrant, uncritical, unselfconscious self-centeredness mixed with compassion as the positive and true foundation of much that appears as lifeless convention. The reader might begin to understand why "there is something very comforting in the utterly banal" (*IP*, 139); the commonplace response may spring from a fundamental goodness manifesting itself without thought to external appearance.

In contrast to Courtesy with her flaming hair and her inadvertent uniqueness is Mrs. Rust. With her hair "dyed a forcible crimson . . . dyed by human agency, . . . she proved the truism that the world takes people at their own valuation" (*IP*, 54—55). But this truism is demonstrably untrue. The initial impression of Mrs. Rust is that she is a forcible woman: independent, headstrong, and unpredictable. The reality of the inner Mrs. Rust is that she is a very ordinary person incapable of originality. "She always said 'good' to everything she had not heard before. To her the newest was of necessity the best. Originality was her ideal, and as unattainable as most ideals are. For she was not in the least original herself. She was doomed for ever to stand outside the door of her temple. And 'good' was her tribute of recognition to those who had free passes into the temple" (*IP*, 62). Most people, including Courtesy, the gardener, the narrator, and the reader, recognize the inner reality of Mrs. Rust in spite of her extravagant exterior. Her dyed hair and admiration for originality reflect her recognition of the benefits of a total immersion in the process of life. Unfortunately, she is unable to muster the innocent selfishness and benevolent amorality necessary to be *in* life. The best she can do is dye her hair, then follow in Courtesy's wake.

Red, the color of life, crowns throbbing lives beneath unimaginative exteriors (Courtesy) and dull lives robed in flamboyant exteriors (Mrs. Rust). But it is also the color of death. The gardener, pinned in the wreckage of the earthquake, notices "a thin and fearful stream of blood that was issuing from two bricks in the mass of miscellany that had once been a house" (*IP*, 137). Mrs. Rust, on the same occasion, sees a man "through a sort of cage of fallen things. It was as if—one had trodden on red currants" (*IP*, 144). But it is flesh and blood, not red currants, that she sees. The flow of red, the color of life, is inevitable at the scene of violent death.

Through a world colored in varying hues of red move the blue figure of the gardener and the gray figure of the suffragette. The gardener is described as a blue man, a man of the sea. The suffragette, on the other hand, was a grey thing, a snake-soul. To the eye of a grey soul there is something forbidding about the many colours of the universe, and you will always know snake-people by their defensive attitude. It is an immensely lonely thing to be a snake, to have that tortuous spirit, with no limbs for contact with the earth. And yet the compensation is most generous, for there are few joys like the joy of knowing yourself alone. (*IP*, 60)

The gray-souled suffragette says that the combination of red and gray is the "most vicious discord" she knows (*IP*, 170). She makes the remark when discussing the Union Town earthquake; she envisions the quaking as red and the pain as gray. Red has been associated with Courtesy, Mrs. Rust, heat, life, and love. Red is the movement of the external world, it is the external reality which contains sun and blood and emotion. For the gray-souled suffragette the quaking which affects the world around her would be red because it is a thing external to herself. Pain is internal, the constant presence by which she knows herself; pain is gray. The gray and red are, for her, a vicious discord because the gray that is her soul could never be part of the red reality of Courtesy, or adopt the red facade of Mrs. Rust.

But why can't there be a union between the gray suffragette and the blue gardener? The gardener attracted by the opal-blue of the sea and the suffragette adoring the opal-gray of the waves are alike in many ways, and the blending of their blue and gray to produce a valuable opal color would seem to be a healthy development of their personalities. Even those aspects of their personalities that seem most incompatible are not irreconcilable. The gardener made his theories and the suffragette's theories made her; a compromise on the issue that contains their most fundamental difference would seem to be beneficial. A balancing of the practical and the ideal should be desirable. In fact, the novel seems for a while to move the characters toward a mutually agreeable union. When the suffragette realizes the extent to which the hypocrisy of Father Christopher is unalterable and unavoidable, the suffering that it mercilessly inflicts upon the women under his "care," her reaction is not to hate men but to seek out the gardener. At the moment when she feels conquered by an "anti," by a force which seems impossible to alter, she, like the gardener before her, realizes that she is not self-sufficient. Her Theory of the Hair Shirt, which demands the renunciation of all comfort and the dedicated pursuit of the ideal, will not suffice to conquer the wrongs that she has set out to right. She feels the human need to find solace with another human: the union of blue and gray seems imminent.

However, by rejecting the Theory of the Hair Shirt and its demand for self-effacement, by beginning the metamorphosis from snake with no limbs for contact with the earth to human with hands reaching out to touch, the suffragette could believe in her own importance not just to others but also to herself. In the process, if she perceives herself as something of consequence, but also as something other than what she believes her real self to be, then the sacrifice of her life for her cause would be, on the one hand, the sacrifice of her most valuable possession in an effort to prove her sincerity, and, on the other hand, the sacrifice of a potentially artificial and lifeless shell for the preservation of personal integrity. Furthermore, with the rejection of the Theory of the Hair Shirt, with the acceptance of the warmth offered by another person, with the commitment to the life envisioned by the gardener, the suffragette must lose her gray soul and acquire a soul of another hue. This idea is made explicit in the final chapter when she returns for a last visit to the Borough and finds she has no place there: "Her heart seemed to take on a different colour as she returned for the last time to the Brown Borough" (*IP*, 305). What color her heart changes to is not specified; however, in light of all that subsequently transpires, it is clear that her heart becomes not opal-colored but yellow: a mustard yellow like the portmanteau she has carried and waved menacingly. Yellow is the color of emptiness and destruction.

During the novel the red of the sun often becomes a world-suffusing yellow, and this fourth color accents the story with important persistence. When the gardener's nasturtium finally blooms, it produces not red flowers the color of Courtesy's hair, as the gardener had hoped, but three yellow flowers. The weight of the yellow blossoms, the "trinity of little gold suns," makes the plant dependent upon a stick which supports the stem. In spite of this assistance the plant, on the alien sea, is eventually killed by the heavy yellow blossoms. The yellow flowers, which are the evidence that the plant is alive and fertile, are also the agents of its destruction. Similarly, the mustard-colored portmanteau which the suffragette carries and alludes to ominously is the most compelling reason for taking her seriously—indeed for noticing her at all. She claims to be able to destroy property with the yellow bag, and the yellow bag with its potential for death defines the life and identity of the militant suffragette.

Once we realize that in her frustration the suffragette is no longer "a grey thing, a snake soul," but instead a creature of yellow, the earlier color patterns in the novel reinforce the impossibility of her union with the gardener. Marriage to the gardener would not produce the valuable opal color; marriage would mean the union of blue and yellow: a combination emblematic of artificiality.

At the beginning of the novel, after the gardener leaves his boarding house, he approaches a blond prostitute covered in the scent of violets. In a hard voice which conveys her awareness that he would not be a good paying customer, this yellow and blue woman rebuffs his advances. The same yellow-blue image reappears when the suffragette admires, and then has to disentangle herself from, a yellow and blue parrot when she first disembarks from the *Caribbeania*. The yellow and blue combination is present in a woman whose acts of "love" are an empty formality endured for the sake of material gain, and in a bird which can mouth words but to whom the sounds are meaningless. Had the suffragette, with her yellow heart and yellow portmanteau, married the gardener, the blue man, their union would have been an empty pose because the person that the suffragette believed herself to be could not exist in the conventional marriage pose. The individual who was the suffragette could not be politely committed to a cause. She must be militant or acquiescent, and she views acquiescence as prison. Rather than acquiesce in the travesty of the union of yellow and blue, the suffragette destroys the shell which once contained her gray self, and in the process destroys the chancel screen bought by a Christian who follows the advice of a priest whose god seems to encourage suffering.

I Pose emphasizes the total isolation of the gardener and the suffragette. They have no names and barely even a hint of a past. The novel highlights the universal isolation of individuals and emphasizes the inescapable destruction that finally resolves the problem of estrangement. Raising questions about personal identity and individual integrity, Stella Benson's first novel is built around the issue of women's rights, but it is the more universal concern for individual life in a world opposed to individuality that makes its theme timeless.

Chapter Four
The Novels of Fantasy

John A. Lester, speaking of the first part of the twentieth century, has observed that "By far, the most prevalent intellectual response of the age, indeed the predominant intellectual attitude in literature, was a resolve to circumvent, or escape from, the confines of that scientific reasoning faculty which seemed to have sprung a deterministic trap for the mind of man . . . . The quests for nonlogical faculties of cognition in this period were many."[1] Nowhere is the quest more clearly charted than in the novels of Stella Benson. Against a background of fantasy her second and third novels grapple with the problem of the disharmony between inner and outer reality, and the very real problem of trying to determine which should be accepted as "true" reality. All of Benson's novels reveal a desperate determination to believe that the individual can establish the terms of his reality. What gives her early novels such force is that at the very moment she is invoking the curative powers of fantasy against unacceptable facts, she recognizes the illusive and elusive nature of fantasy.

I Pose ended with a question. *This Is the End* opens with a declaration, an assertion of belief in the nonfactual. The narrator is explicit: there is a life of the heart accessible to everyone, which is more important than the external world confronting the body. The narrator's assertion would sound like frightened whistling in the dark were it not for the impossible and improbable facts the reader accepts while reading the novel. The story of Jay in *This Is the End* emphasizes the fragility of the inner life, while revealing that it exists, or existed at one time, in everyone. Irreconcilable inconsistencies within the novel support the world view that there *is* a truth that all the reasoning in the world cannot verify but that may be discovered by anyone.

The third novel, *Living Alone*, reiterates the idea of the reality of fantasy, but both inner and outer worlds seem bleak and lonely. Paradoxically, *Living Alone* is both more fantastic and more realistic than its predecessors.

This Is the End

In 1917 the book reviewer of the *Dial* asked his readers to "Imagine a book that starts like an essay on modern philosophy, continues like a

The Novels of Fantasy

confession, goes at a bound into fiction, shifts into the manner of a Kipling fairy tale, and ends in perfect consistency with them all."[2] In this way he introduced them to Stella Benson's second novel, *This Is the End*. The narrator begins the novel by explaining:

This is the end, for the moment, of all thinking, this is my unfinal conclusion. There is no reason in tangible things, and no system in the ordinary ways of the world. Hands were made to grope, and feet to stumble, and the only things you may count on are the unaccountable things. System is a fairy and a dream, you never find system where or when you expect it. There are no reasons except reasons you and I don't know.

. . . I feel no security in facts, precedent seems no protection to me . . . .

But if the things which I know in spite of my education were false, if the eyes of the sea forgot their secret, or if the accent of the steep woods became vulgar, if the fairy adventures that happen in my heart fell flat, if the good friends my eyes have never seen failed me,—then indeed should I know emptiness, and an astonishment that would kill.[3]

The protagonist of the novel has also lived a life of the imagination; not until the fairy adventures of her heart have been exiled by facts does she surrender to marriage and the everyday, reasonable world.

Jay (Jane Elizabeth Martin) is a "Suffragetty" sort of girl "wasting an expensive education" working in London as a bus conductor. She sends her Family (Benson's capitalization) letters describing her dream life in a house on a cliff by the sea, but writes about this life as though it were fact. There are four other members of Jay's Family: her beloved brother Kew, who is home on leave from the war (WW I); Cousin Gustus, approaching seventy and a dedicated pessimist; his wife, a woman novelist of forty-five known in the family as Anonyma; and her newly acquired satellite, Mr. Russell, whose wife is off in America working for peace. When the Family sets off in search of Jay, Kew knows she is living in London but has promised not to reveal this fact. Anonyma, armed with her road map, intends to track down the clues to the Secret World in which, the reader is told, four-fifths of Jay lives. Cousin Gustus goes, convinced as always that the worst possible event will result from each action taken. Mr. Russell drives his car Christina and is ignored by all. Mr. Russell, however, knows far more than even he suspects. He knows Jay, but does not realize that the girl he has just met is the girl he is looking for. Furthermore, neither Jay nor Mr. Russell realizes until too late that Mr. Russell is Jay's Secret Friend in her Secret World. The Secret World was once Mr. Russell's dream also, and he somehow, without realizing it until he arrives, drives to the place where the Secret House used to stand.

From the moment Mr. Russell discovers where the Secret House used to stand, Jay's Secret World begins to slip inexplicably from her. Her confrontation with reality intensifies when she meets Mr. Russell so that he may deliver a message from Kew, who has returned to the front. After delivering Kew's message, Mr. Russell tells Jay that he has found the House by the Sea. She tries to silence him: "Don't tell me facts, because I know they will bar me for ever out of my House by the Sea. Facts are contraband there." But Mr. Russell announces, "There is no House by that Sea now." Because he was "not sufficiently alive to be observant . . . he did not know that she was unhappy" (*TITE*, 213−14). So Mr. Russell single-mindedly nails down the Secret World with facts.

When Jay returns to London after this conversation with Mr. Russell, she discovers William Morgan, her ex-fiancé, waiting for her with the news that her brother Kew has been killed. The inescapable intrusion of facts from the physical world into her secret world, the certain knowledge that there was once such a house as her Secret House but that it is now gone and its site occupied by a slate quarry, and the finality of her brother's absence—these forces from the physical world invade and destroy the secret world and drive Jay into the arms of conventional William Morgan who, believing that he lies, promises he will never die. In truth, the William Morgans of the world, safe and sensible, are in a sense immortal. On their conventional strength the world depends for war and for comfort.

The prose section of the book ends with a dialogue entitled "Anti-Climax." Anonyma, who knows nothing of what has passed between Jay and Mr. Russell, is commenting to him on her niece's marriage to a likable, conventional, perfectly acceptable young man.

"It is well," sighed Anonyma, "that our little Jay has at last found Romance. Since first she came to my arms—toddling sceptic of four—I have seen what she lacked, I have prayed that I—who possessed it—might perhaps be inspired to give her the Clue. . . . Yet to young Bill Morgan it was given to show her the way . . . to unlock the door. . . . Oh! Russ, we grow older and wiser and are left behind. The young reap where we have sown. . . . Is this always to be the end of our youth?"

Mr. Russell laughed a little. "Yes," he said. "This is the end." (*TITE*, 241−42; ellipses in text)

There follows a poem that describes mortality as the compensation for humanity: perfection may be unattainable, but as consolation humans understand that life in this imperfect world will not endure forever.

However, it is quite important to remember the opening paragraphs before closing the adventure of the novel with a sigh and a "Well! so that's the way it is." Mr. Russell's final comment may reflect the truth as he sees it and as Anonyma believes it, but it is not the truth that the narrator believes. Thus, the reader is encouraged to adopt at least one of Jay's characteristics and end his thoughts on a questioning note.

Both the theme and the characters in this novel are developed through gentle but highly effective irony. For instance, the significance of the "Anti-Climax" may be missed if the reader forgets the narrator's initial assertion that it is her faith in the insubstantial nature of fact that allows her to continue living. The dichotomy between the opening and closing sentiments must be recognized. The narrator's assertion denies the inevitability as well as the desirability of the complete capitulation to reality which seems to be the final fate of each of the characters in this novel.

The narrator discusses the characters with precisely controlled omniscience. Statements that initially appear to be reflections of the narrator's opinion often prove to be, upon careful reading, her transmission of the impression the characters make upon others. When she makes factual observations about the characters, the facts are demonstrably accurate in light of the character's actions; however, what often becomes apparent is that these facts are not the *truth* of these people. The real people cannot be understood through memorization of a list of facts.

The reader learns that Mrs. Gustus, known in the Family as Anonyma, "prided herself on simplicity. Spelt with a Capital S, it constituted her Diety." But the reader is also told that

> to be simple is all very well, but turn it into an active verb and you spoil the whole idea. To simplify seems forced, and I think Mrs. Gustus struck harder on the note of simplification than that of simplicity. . . . Her age was five-and-forty, and . . . she was a novelist . . . but she had an imperceptible earthly public. She wrote laborious books, full of short peevish sentences, of such very pure construction that they were extremely difficult to understand. She wore spectacles with aggressive tortoise-shell rims. She said, "I am short-sighted. I am obliged to wear spectacles. Why should I try to conceal the fact? I will not have a pair of rimless ghosts haunting my face. I will wear spectacles without shame." But the real truth was that the tortoise-shell rims were more becoming to her. (*TITE*, 8–9).

Anonyma's unselfconscious pose is consciously adopted and clearly revealed by the narrator as a pose.

When the narrator, explaining Anonyma's views of Jay, says "It was too much to ask her [Anonyma]—a professional theory maker—to adapt her theories to the young and literal. That was the worst of Jay, she was so literal, so unimaginative, so lacking in the simple unpractical quality of poetry" (*TITE*, 70), there are several layers of irony. A person who prides herself on simplicity should, one would suppose, speak quite literally. Yet it is Jay's literal acceptance of her theories that annoys Anonyma. Further, she believes Jay, four-fifths of whose life is spent in her Secret World, is unimaginative and "so lacking in the simple unpractical quality of poetry." Not only is Anonyma's judgment of Jay erroneous, but also her judgment of poetry might well be called into doubt. It has been said that it is poetry that makes life beautiful, and there is a practical necessity for beauty if life is to be worth living. Anonyma is a maker of theories whose surface compliance with her theories reveals an imaginative failure to grasp the truth of her own theories.

Yet Anonyma, who goes to great lengths to simplify, is revealed in her human complexity. When the reader first learns that she patterned herself after the heroines in her books, the reader might silently mock this posturing shortsighted woman. However, for all her posturing and quite pretentious minor ministrations to the poor—all of which are transparently inconsequential—she does, when faced with what she genuinely believes to be a dangerous situation, attempt to capture a man she believes is a German spy. The fact that he turns out to be a Quaker trying to capture her in the mistaken belief that *she* is a spy makes for comedy but does not alter the reality that she was willing to risk personal danger for her country. Furthermore, the seemingly undaunted Anonyma is spied confiding to the indifferent sea, "It is much more delightful to be intelligent than to be beautiful" (*TITE*, 156). The fact that she misses on both counts inspires a compassion in the reader for her vulnerability. This enormous woman "conceived on a generous scale" (*TITE*, 8) becomes a mocking exaggeration of the good, perceptive, articulate woman she would like to be. Anonyma, who had, may even still have, a Secret World of her own, fails to recognize the presence of a Secret World in others. When she says of Jay's House by the Sea, "We know very little about it except that it exists" (*TITE*, 80), what she is saying is true, though not literally factual. The House is real to Jay and to Mr. Russell, and it did once exist in the world of the external fact. But the one thing Anonyma is certain of, that there is now a physical building answering the description in Jay's letters, is not an accurate statement of fact.

Although Anonyma's husband, Cousin Gustus, is a bitter, depressing man, "he was very well provided with human affections, and . . . he loved Kew better than any one else in the world" (*TITE*, 150). A glimpse of the depth of emotion concealed by a morbid exterior does not become a sentimental memory for the reader because it is followed immediately by a marvelous caricature of Cousin Gustus as the mindless proponent of the "God-is-on-our-side; the-enemy-is-the-depraved-agent-of-the-devil" attitude. The reader's laughter as Cousin Gustus's rhetorical questions prove to be logical farces which can only be answered in a manner exactly opposite to his intention, as he condemns what turn out to be England's actions, echoes against the wall of grief that has brought on his outburst: Kew has just returned to the front.

"Kew's going has upset me so that my headache has returned, and I cannot get any Aspirin here," continued Cousin Gustus. "I know a man who was very much addicted to these neuralgic headaches, who committed suicide by throwing himself from the bathroom window, solely owing to neuralgia. And the rain does nothing towards improving matters. They say the German guns bring on the rain. I tell you there is no limit to their guilt. Look at this morning's paper: 'The enemy bombarded this section of our front with increasing intensity during the day . . .' I ask you, IS THAT WAR?"
"Yes," said Mr. Russell absently.
"Nonsense," said Cousin Gustus. "What we ought to do is to shoot every German we can catch. Shooting's too good for them. Hang them. That would teach them. Any Government but ours would have thought of it long ago." (*TITE*, 151–52)

Cousin Gustus's deep concern for Kew is played against the comic background of his ready supply of tales of disaster and his unthinking and all-embracing condemnation of Germans and Germany. The reader can neither wholly accept him as a harmless old man talking to hide his fear for the safety of a loved one, nor wholly condemn him as a brutal, unthinking jingoist capable of considering all outsiders subhuman.

Both Cousin Gustus and his wife Anonyma seem at first to be shallow and disagreeable, yet each eventually elicits sympathy even from an initially unsympathetic reader. It is important to notice the positive aspects of the characters in the novel because the reader should realize that there is no particular "type" of person that is inherently admirable. In *This Is the End* Benson offers what Anonyma would call "word vignettes," rather than what the modern critic would call well-rounded characters. Yet these characters are dynamic enough to throw the reader repeatedly off balance when he believes he understands them. The reader is constantly forced to recognize the "unfinal" nature of his own conclusions.

Although Jay, Kew, Anonyma, Cousin Gustus, Mr. Russell, and his wife are very dissimilar, they all have one thing in common: they all seem to live in isolation even though they are part of an ostensibly closeknit group. It is Mr. Russell, the man most obviously an outsider, who seems to have something in common with all the other family members. Yet he is so self-absorbed that just when the reader might expect him to understand and be understood—during his final meeting with Jay—he loses all possibility of reentering what was once his Secret World because he fails to grasp the insubstantial nature of that world. He attempts to demonstrate its reality by defining it with facts, and in doing so he underscores for the reader the essential isolation of the human condition. Mr. Russell is oblivious to Jay and her emotions at the very moment when he is trying to convince her that he is in fact her Secret Friend, the guardian-companion in the Secret World with whom she should presumably be able to find comfort in the world of reality.

The reader is alerted early to the probability of unappreciated qualities in Mr. Russell. The narrator introduces him sympathetically, explaining that Mr. Russell had

only lately been culled by Mrs. Gustus—that assiduous collector—and placed in the bosom of the Family. She had found him blossoming unloved in the wilderness of a War Work Committee. He was well informed, yet a good listener. . . . He had no sense of humour, but hid this deformity skillfully. Hardly anybody knew that he was a poet, except presumably his dog. He often talked to his dog; he told it every speakable thought that he had. This was his only bad habit. Occasionally his dog was heard to reply in a small curious voice proceeding also from Mr. Russell. (*TITE*, 11, 13)

The poetry in Mr. Russell might be the poetry in all people, a potential; in him as in many others, it is a poetry unrealized. Mr. Russell himself fails to recognize the powers of his imagination although the reader moves toward the belief that there is something fine but undeveloped in him. He is revealed as "The victim of an unwitty cynicism, and of a heavy irresponsibility. . . . He knew within himself that Life was made of paper, and thrown together in a crackling chaos. . . . The only thing that ever made his heart laugh was the idea of fineness finding place in himself. A dream of himself in a heroic light sometimes made him poke himself in the ribs, and mock the farce of human vanity. He was like a man in a world that lacked mirrors, a man who sees his dark deformed shadow on the sands, and thinks it represents him fairly" (*TITE*, 89, 110). This man with no sense of humor finds humor in the thought of fineness in himself. Though there may be or may have been a fineness in him (and the last sentence in the passage above certainly indicates there is), the fineness unrecognized has never flowered and he no longer even suspects its existence.

He once had a Secret World but has lost it twice. The first time he grew old and lost the Secret World of his youth. After rediscovering it through Jay, he loses it again because he insists on verifying the factual foundation upon which it was built. He has lost the power of fantasy and so is lost in the world of facts. In the world of facts he is considered a good conversationalist because he never speaks. Mr. Russell, who seems to have an inner life of significance, is in fact an empty husk because he cannot recognize his own poetic perception of extra-rational truth. Thus, while attempting to clutch fantasy too tightly, he squeezes it dry.

If Mr. Russell eventually confirms his emptiness in spite of early hints of inner complexity, then Kew, who seems to the passer-by to have little depth, is finally and perhaps in spite of himself the propounder of the ultimate riddle. The narrator is careful to introduce him as a young man in whom there *seems* to be an absence of mystery.

His eye and his ear and his mind were all equally slow to appreciate clashings of any kind. He was rather aloof from comparison and criticism, but not on principle. He had no principles—at least no original ones, just the ordinary stuffy old principles of decency and all that. . . . He never turned his eyes inward, as far as the passer-by could see; he lived in a breezy life outside himself. He never tried to make a fine Kew of himself; he never propounded riddles to his Creator, which is the way most of us make our reputations. (*TITE*, 11)

In this passage the narrator's technique of ironic disclosure is, in retrospect, quite clear. "Equally slow" is probably first understood by the reader to mean "not fast." Not until later does the reader remember that "equally slow" is synonymous with "equally fast." The narrator has simply said Kew's eyes, ears, and mind work together. Kew's "ordinary stuffy old principles of decency and all that" are far from usual. He does not grudgingly follow conventional rules of decency; rather, he lives the spirit of decency. His principles have become clichés for many people who are unable to follow them; Kew is unusual in that he unthinkingly, unpretentiously, and sincerely embraces those principles.

Although it is Kew's pretense "never to do anything on principle" (*TITE*, 128) he is revealed in truth as a man whose principles are so fundamental that he is naturally good. As the narrator explains it: "He was so simple he did his best without thinking about it" (*TITE*, 129). But simple in Kew's case is not synonymous with "easy to understand."

He is simple in that he preserves an amoral innocence. The reader learns that Kew is an accomplished and unrepentant liar, and the reader approves of his lies. For instance, when Kew realizes that Jay is determined not to return home, he asks her to embellish her letters with false clues to her whereabouts so that Anonyma may derive some pleasure from the lies as she attempts to track them down. On another occasion, telling Jay he must return to the front, he assures her that he could not be killed because the idea of death assulting his "Me" was unthinkable: after all, "I'm too average a man to get killed" (*TITE*, 126). Yet later, he prepared the rest of the Family for the eventuality of his death and deliberately left them with the memory of a patriotic young man going off to face his future, jaunty and confident that death would not be so horrible a calamity. His lies are never self-serving. Because he always hopes his minor deceptions will comfort or cheer essentially lonely people, he is remembered as a good person, not a mendacious one.

Kew, who never seemed to look inward and examine himself, is revealed as a complex man capable of significant self-awareness and self-control. Dying, he reassures his friend that he does not mind dying because death will be a relief from the self that he knows too well. To console Jay, he sends her the message that "death was just an ordinary old thing, no more romantic than anything else" (*TITE*, 226). But then, just how romantic *is* everything else for Kew? Reinforcing the reader's awareness of Kew's many contradictions are his last words, overheard by William Morgan: "This is awfully exciting" (*TITE*, 231). Kew, who never posed riddles for his creator, is the riddle the reader must solve. So fundamentally honest though an accomplished liar, so perceptive though apparently oblivious, so intent on deromanticizing while naturally heroic, he seems both a promise that a sustained life of the imagination is possible and a warning that if life does not kill the imagination death will take the body that houses it. It is in the apparently practical Kew that a selflessness is manifest; he is conscious of and considerate of the needs of everyone around him. He is well liked by all and apparently at peace with himself. Yet in his dying effort to console a friend he leads the reader to suspect unhappiness, dissatisfaction, and self-doubt in this "simple" young man.

The reality of Kew and the reality of Mr. Russell finally confront Jay. Their realities, although Kew encourages imaginative flights and Mr. Russell wishes to share them, finally blind her with fact and destroy her Secret World.

The reader rapidly becomes aware that the "suffragetty" Jay is not a carefree spirit off on the heady adventure of life. The deadly routine of her job and the consequent feeling of alienation from her surroundings produce a despair she only temporarily escapes in the Secret World. Though the nearest she ever gets to joy is in her Secret World, this world also contains mind-arresting, heart-stopping terror which has caused more than one "natural" death in the real world of London. Jay's refuge, with its beauty and terror, infringes upon the real world and is in turn affected by it. In spite of its enormous effect upon her life, the reality of Jay's fantasy is not safe, and in fact, and because of fact, the Secret World is eventually lost in spite of Jay's desire to retain it.

In the early decades of the twentieth century there was considerable consternation about the handling of sexual matters in novels and the growing tendency to leave "fallen" heroines relatively unpunished. One critic of *This Is the End* declared that the novel seemed but another venture into amorality with a young woman apparently intent upon an extramarital liaison with a married man.[4] However, the bond between Jay and Mr. Russell is so sexless, and the intended moonlight rendezvous is so asexual that the reader is hard-pressed to envision just what would happen had Jay kept the appointment. This is, after all, the story of the fate of the unseen and unprovable in the real world, and the meeting of Jay and her secret friend would be much more likely to have resulted in the reappearance of the magic house by the sea with its innocence and terrors than in the sexual union that would have sealed irrevocably the way to the secret world. And of course, Jay does not in fact go to meet the married Mr. Russell at the site of the house by the sea; therefore, she is clearly not a fallen woman.

Furthermore, the marriage which marks the end of the novel is not a reward for a virtuous heroine but a defeat of youth, romance, and dreams. Bill Martin, Jay's husband-to-be, is mentioned only twice: once at the beginning of the novel to establish that Jay had earlier firmly declined his proposal and has had no regrets about her decision, and once at the end when he delivers the news that Jay's brother has been killed and offers himself as comfort to the desolated and isolated Jay. Jay's marriage to conventional Bill Martin ensures her isolation from her own inner world.

The suffragette in *I Pose* committed suicide rather than succumb to the temptation of a marriage that she feared would become a tomb for her personal identity. Instead of rejecting the conventional ending for a heroine who has not behaved immorally, *This Is the End* reveals the threadbare reward that marriage can be. But Benson is not content with simply demonstrating the absence of passion with which a young girl sinks into matrimony; through Cousin Gustus and Mr. Russell she attacks a pervasive romantic myth of the ideal husband: the kindly, experienced, older man.

Early in the nineteenth century Jane Austen's Emma certainly needed the guidance of wise and patient Mr. Knightly, and Charlotte Bronte's Jane Eyre, sheltered but strong-willed, was understandably attracted to the experienced and forceful Mr. Rochester. The convention of the desirable older husband was so strong that when George Eliot in *Middlemarch* exposed the barrenness that often results from a marriage in which the husband is considerably older than the wife, the lesson was lost upon thousands of readers and hundreds of writers. Well into the twentieth century the convention continued that an older man is a highly desirable marriage partner for a young woman. Whether the father figure in *Rebecca of Sunnybrook Farm* or the byronic hero in Daphne DuMaurier's *Rebecca*, older men are seen as romantic, protective, desirable husbands. This sentimental myth, still flourishing on bookstands today (see, for example, the Harlequin romances), is rejected in *This Is the End*.

Cousin Gustus seems more in need of a nurse companion than a wife. Anonyma, fifteen years younger than her husband, is so starved for affection that she resorts to enlarging the family circle by acquiring equally lonely strangers. Yet life with a querulous husband has taught her to withhold genuine commitment, so her relationship with Mr. Russell is essentially impersonal and her contact with the poor serves no purpose beyond allowing her to record in her diary real and imagined bits of dialogue. As further attack on the myth of the ideal older husband, Mr. Russell, the older man who was Jay's secret friend in her Secret World, becomes, when she faces him, a real person: not a strong father-lover but a lonely, middle-aged man so intent upon securing comfort for himself that he is completely oblivious to the real needs of the person who is looking to him for protection from the world.

Benson's point was not that marriage is inevitably bad, but that marriage is not inevitably good. It is a tribute to her accomplishment that without offering any suggestion that Bill Martin will be a bad husband, she nonetheless conveys the sense of loss that accompanies the acceptance of the standard role for a woman. It would have been quite easy to give this fine young man a hint of vice or unworthiness; few would doubt that a bad husband can bring a lifetime of grief to a woman. But Benson develops the realistic observation that husbands (or wives) do not necessarily bring happiness and contentment. Neither Cousin Gustus nor Mr. Russell is happily married even though the first clearly has a wife who was (maybe still is) alive to the world around her, and the second is himself a man who once had an active life of the imagination. Neither has found a soul mate; and neither apparently will Jay, even though she has been claimed by a young man who cares for her. In the world of Benson's novels love is not the solvent for loneliness.

In *This Is the End* the narrator explains "there is only one thing that can adequately usurp the place of Peace. But its name did not occur to Jay" (*TITE*, 177). When Jay spends a great deal of time thinking about Mr. Russell, finds "irresponsible wants" clamoring in her breast, and in quick trips to the Secret World feels expectant rather than simply content, the reader suspects that love is beginning to adequately usurp the place of peace. Unfortunately, love, even when it exists, is not a cure-all. Mr. Russell not only does not bring her any comfort, he is the primary agent in the destruction of the Secret World which had offered Jay's imagination an escape from the real world drudgery that confronted her. To emphasize the idea that love cannot be a cure for loneliness, Benson sends Jay out with a dimunitive woman named Mrs. Love as her drinking companion when her Secret World fails her. It is Mrs. Love who explains that they are "temp'ary pals right enough, there ain't no permanent kind" (*TITE*, 191). Neither Mrs. Love nor Mr. Russell can replace the Secret World, and Jay recognizes that "there are only dreams, to keep our souls alive. We are lucky if we get good dreams. We'll never get anything better. . . . There is nothing in the world but second bests, but dreams are an excellent second best" (*TITE*, 193). But even her dreams fail her.

This Is the End might lead one to conclude that fantasy *cannot* withstand the assault of reality. But the novel argues not only for the continuing necessity for fantasy, but for the possibility of salvation from reality provided by the mind that is determined to secure its Secret World. Stella Benson was writing during a time when the reality of war was proving to be a horror nearly unimaginable a decade earlier. When the narrator asks, "Oh, friend of childlike mind, what is it that these years have taken from us, what is it that we have lost, oh friend, besides contentment?" (*TITE*, 77), the answer is "innocence." The answer is dramatized in an incident that occurs during the search for Jay.

Directed to a house by the sea which seems to be clearly not what they are looking for, the Family become involved in a discussion with the owner, a deaf old woman: "Anonyma noticed that her hair was apparently done in imitation of a pigeon's nest, also that many hooks at the back of her dress had lost their grip of the situation" (*TITE*, 89). This comic figure explains the toys that populate the yard and house as the first deployment of her preparations for the return of her son Murray, who is coming home on leave from the war and has written to say that he wants to forget the war and play civilian games with her when he returns. Her detailed discussion of how she and her son used to play together and her careful explanation of the functions of the many natural props in their make-believe world are followed by Kew, who becomes increasingly restless as he becomes more involved in her explanations. He finally writes on her slate,

"I am very much afraid that all leave from abroad has been stopped this week."

"Yes, I know," said the mother, "I have been unhappy about that for some days. But it doesn't make any difference to Murray now. You see, I heard last night that he was killed on Tuesday. That's why I know he will come, and I shall be waiting here. Can't you imagine them shouting as they get through, as they get through with being grown-up, shouting to each other as they run back to their childhood and their old pretences. . . ."

After a moment she added, "That is the only sound that I shall ever hear now,—the shouting of Murray to me as he runs home."

It was in a sort of dream that Kew watched Anonyma go forward and take both the hands of the mother. I suppose he knew that all that was superfluous, and that Murray would come home.

. . .

Kew was not sorry that he had intruded. (*TITE*, 94–95)

The deaf old woman, who takes what life has given her, will live in her Secret World with Murray. Death has not stolen either her contentment or her innocence, and the first seems to have been dependent upon the second. Because Murray would live only in her Secret World, she would never have to face a Murray she did not understand, or who was not just the way she wanted him to be.

The world of *This Is the End* is occupied by unhappy humans, unable either to communicate their own grief or to understand another's. Mr. Russell, who once occupied Jay's Secret World as her Secret Friend, fails to notice when she is unhappy, so he cannot understand the cause of her dismay. The narrator, even with her faith in Secret Worlds maintained, accepts them as worlds of detachment and isolation. When in her Secret World, the narrator is no more than "a thin column of air." She neither participates in nor fully understands the nature of the life of the Secret World. As she explains it, "you pass through the place as a ghost, your bubble enchantment encloses you, your Secret Friends have no knowledge of you, their story runs without you. Your unnecessary identity is tactfully ignored, and you know the heaven of being dispassionate and detached among things you love" (*TITE*, 6).

Benson's narrator welcomes the isolation of a Secret World strikingly similar to John Keats's in "Ode to a Nightingale." The poem records a series of lovely but lonely images until finally the narrator imagines

> . . . magic casements, opening on the foam
> Of perilous seas in faery lands forlorn.
>
> Forlorn! the very word is like a bell
> To toll me back from thee to my sole self!
> Adieu! the fancy cannot cheat so well
> As she is fam'd to do, deceiving elf.
> . . .
> Was it a vision or a waking dream?

The very detachment and solitude that drives Keats's narrator back to his "sole self" in the external world is the comfort of the Secret World for Benson's narrator. In the world of her imagination there is a freedom from emotional responsibility and individual identity. Such freedom does not appeal to everyone, and may not be able to be maintained by a sympathetic, compassionate person in a real world full of lonely people. In the real world we are all besieged by requests, articulate and inarticulate, for comfort or recognition. Freedom from the real demands of humanity, including one's own need for love, may be but an enchanting dream; and to this dream as we become more entangled with those around us, we are less and less able to escape.

This Is the End is not the best of Benson's novels, but its weaknesses actually contribute to the development of the intellectual message of the work. Apparent inconsistencies develop a well-wrought reflection of the incomprehensible world that confronts a sensibility finer than Mr. Russell's, a soul more determined than Jay's. *This Is the End* both insists that there is an essential extra-rational element in our lives and acknowledges that that element is fatally vulnerable when attacked by fact. Jay's marriage, her capitulation to convention, seems proof of the truth of Mr. Russell's final conclusion—there is an inevitable end of dreams, or of Keats's assertion that "the fancy cannot cheat so well / As she is fam'd to do." But Benson's narrator, with her "unfinal conclusion," seems to assert throughout the novel that it is not the failure of imagination but the failure of the will to imagine that establishes the falsehood of fantasy.

Living Alone

Benson's third novel, populated with witches, wizards, flying broomsticks, fairies, and dragons is more emphatically a fantasy than the first two. Yet the novel confronts an unromantic reality in a way the others do not. The heroines in Benson's first two novels are allowed an unusual choice. The usual dilemma of women in fiction was not *whether* to marry but whom to marry or how to marry. By permitting the heroines of her first two novels to elect not to marry, Benson was departing from the approved conventional plot. However, she was unable to offer a vision of the life of an unmarried woman. A pleasant life for a woman of no particular talent (usually in novels the talent was novel writing) who had chosen not to marry was unimaginable. Significantly, the suffragette had to eliminate herself altogether if she were to resist marriage. Jay, on the other hand, once rejected marriage, then finally relented. In *Living Alone* Benson explores the life of a single woman who does not regret her husbandless condition. Like Graham Greene's Major Scobie in *The Heart of the Matter*, some people—women included—might prefer the peace of loneliness to the pain that often attends intimate relationships. Such a woman is Sarah Brown. She is unmarried and neither particularly attractive nor particularly attracted to anyone, man or woman.

Living Alone is the story of Sarah Brown's life after she meets a witch. Sarah Brown is a faceless and nearly nameless member of a charity committee; the witch is the superintendent of a store and boarding house known as the House of Living Alone. Boarders in the House of Living Alone pay no rent, but must agree to observe rules enforcing almost complete seclusion and must resist any temptation to make their lodging "homey." Sarah Brown moves into the House of Living Alone with her one companion, David the Dog. The only other lodger is Peony, an "unmarried wife," who tells Sarah Brown about Albert, a magic boy who led her to the father of the child she is expecting in May, a child she knows will be Albert.

Under the influence of a magic sandwich, Sarah Brown quits her job "in a small office, collecting evidence from charitable spies about the Naughty poor,"[5] and leaves to seek love in the world outside. Needing to support herself, she finds a job working on a farm superintended by an ineffectual dragon whose weak commands are blithely ignored by the fairy fieldhands. Unused to strenuous activity, Sarah is soon conquered by the physical pain attendant upon the unfamiliar outdoor work and is returned to the House of Living Alone by the wizard Richard. Meanwhile, the witch has been seen battling a German witch over London and is sought by the police. Believing the witch in danger of arrest, Sarah Brown insists the witch accompany her to the United States. Just as their ship passes the Statue of Liberty, the witch returns to England. The novel ends as Sarah Brown, deaf and alone, enters the United States, "the greater House of Living Alone."

The reader may feel a certain tragic finality as Sarah Brown enters the United States completely deaf and abandoned by the witch. But Sarah has really lost nothing. The witch accompanied her across the ocean out of curiosity not out of love, and Sarah left behind no one who would miss her. In a new, unmagic land she will be locked within herself—but then, she always has been. She chose to live in the House of Living Alone. She preferred the loneliness and occasional terror of solitude to the comfort of human contact. Though her inner life may not accord with what is usually considered desirable, it is the life she prefers. Her deafness is a barrier to human contact, but it is neither insurmountable nor necessarily bad. Murray's mother in *This Is the End* was deaf, and the physical disability was an asset in the perpetuation of her life of the imagination. As the witch explained to Sarah Brown, "as long as you can hear magic you will not lack a key to your prison. Sometimes it's better not to hear the other things" (*LA*, 37).

Living Alone is a novel of fantasy; yet it addresses the real issue of isolation in the real world. The heroine has no resource beyond herself; she looks forward to no significant future work for which she is sacrificing or even enduring now; she has no warm memories of any specific past accomplishment to which her life has been devoted. She is a less dramatic version of the suffragette in *I Pose*. True, she is the doer of committees: she, like the suffragette, performs the tedious and unromantic chores required for any movement to move. But, unlike the suffragette, she seems to work not out of any sense of deliberately submitting her pride, but out of a sense that such tasks are the only ones appropriate for her. Furthermore, she has neither the dedicated sense of mission of the suffragette nor the despondent sense that all is not as it should be which haunted Jay in *This Is the End*. Sarah Brown seems to move through a world in which she neither feels she is a citizen nor desires to be one.

However, Sarah Brown's strong sense of duty does not render her insensitive to the inadequacy of indifferent charity unaccompanied by sympathetic response. The narrator explains that "high on the list of crimes possible to Registrars and Workers" in charity offices is sentimentality.

It is sentimental to feel personal affection for a Case, or to give a child of the Naughty Poor a penny without full enquiry, or to say "A-goo" to a grey pensive baby eating dirt on the pavement, or to acknowledge the right of a Case to ask questions sometimes instead of answering them, or to disapprove of spying and tale-bearing, or to believe any statement made by any one without an assured income, or to quote any part of the New Testament, or in fact to confuse in any way the ideas of charity and love. Christ, who, by the way, unfortunately omitted to join any reputable philanthropic society, commanded seekers of salvation to be poor and to despise themselves. But this was sentimental, and the Charity Society decrees that only the prosperous and the self-respectful shall deserve a hearing. (*LA*, 87).

Under the influence of a magic powder Sarah Brown succumbs to the temptation of sentimentality and realizes "real Love knows her neighbor face to face, and laughs with him and weeps with him, and eats and drinks with him, so that at last, when his black day dawns, she may share with him, not what she can spare, but all that she has" (*LA*, 92). And so Sarah Brown leaves the office of "greedy Charity" and goes out to confront "Love and April outside the window" (*LA*, 94). That Sarah Brown never can confront love herself creates the poignancy of the book; that she misses love through her disinclination to confront life arrests the incipient pathos.

Although Sarah Brown never develops an exclusive love for anyone, she is nonetheless capable of unselfish acts for others. She left England for the United States for the sole purpose of protecting the witch from arrest. A policeman had come looking for the owner of an unlicensed flying machine seen above London during an air raid. Believing the jaws of the law were about to close, Sarah insisted the witch accompany her out of the country. In this episode Benson brings home the problem of communication and understanding. As the ship arrives in the United States the witch confesses that she had accompanied Sarah out of curiosity: she wanted to see just how evil Sarah would be. When she finally realizes that Sarah's harsh orders were meant to protect, that there was no desire either to rob the witch of her power or to insist that the power be used for selfish ends, she confesses that she had been mistaken in her judgment. At the same time the witch announces that she must leave at once. The United States is a land devoid of magic; Sarah Brown must enter alone. Thus, attempting to help, Sarah finds her actions totally misinterpreted. When she points out to the witch that she will be friendless in a strange land, the witch reminds her that she has always preferred solitude.

Sarah Brown has no burning public or private purpose in life, she simply does not prefer close contact with other people. Benson never gives her an opportunity to choose whether to marry (presumably the preferred destiny of all women), but Benson does let the reader see that marriage holds no attraction for Sarah Brown. Sarah envys the lot of no one and is attracted to none of the men. Even when she thinks about the wizard Richard she thinks "not of Richard's Richard, but of some pale private Richard of her own" (LA, 181). When Richard, emerging with her from the Enchanted Forest, begins to exclaim "Love—," he apologizes explaining "I thought I was talking to my True Love." She replies "I'm sorry you weren't. I mean, I'm sorry it was only me you were talking to" (LA, 193). With that the problem of communication comes squarely home to the reader. Does she mean she wishes for Richard's sake that he were with his true love? Or that she wishes she were the person who is his true love? The answer is probably a combination of these responses, a combination which Sarah Brown herself might not recognize. But Sarah Brown will never really need to decide the exact meaning of her statement; she can retreat to her own world where her imagination projects the realized wish before the desire is consciously expressed. "All the best things that she remembered had only happened in her dreams, her imagination no sooner sipped the first sip of an experience than it conjured up for her grand absurd satisfying draughts of nectar, for which the waking Sarah Brown might thirst in vain. But there was no waking Sarah Brown. Her life was only a sleep-walking; only very rarely did she wake for a moment and feel ashamed to see how alert was the world around her" (LA, 181). Her imagination offers all that she wants while it preserves her solitude. The solitude holds loneliness—a welcome loneliness. Even during life's more vulnerable moments, during incapacity caused by painful illness, when most of mankind might prefer to be attended, Sarah Brown prefers solitude.

Sarah accepts herself as she is. She does not judge herself by others' standards—a truly remarkable independence even in today's literature. She accepts full responsibility for any unhappiness she may feel, but though alone, she does not seem particularly unhappy. She does not see herself as misunderstood and therefore neglected, or in any way injured by human agency. She is what she is, and though she indulges in some mild railing against fate, she takes pride in what she has done with what fate, or heaven, has given her:

Heaven has given me wretched health, but never gave me youth enough to make the wretchedness adventurous. . . . Health gave me a thin skin, but never gave me the natural and comforting affections. Heaven probably meant to make a noble woman of me by encrusting me in disabilities, but it left out, in fact, all the compensations. But luckily I have found the compensations for myself: I just had to find something. Men and women have given me everything that such as I could expect. I have never met with reasonless enmity, never met with meanness, never met with anything more unbearable than natural indifference, from any man or woman. I have been, I may say, a burden and a bore all over the world; I have been an ill and fretful stranger within all men's gates; I have asked much and given nothing; I have never been a friend. Nobody has ever expected any return from me, yet nothing was grudged. Landladies, policemen, chorus girls, social bounders, prostitutes, the natural enemies, one would say, of such as I, have given me kindness, and often much that they could not easily spare, and always amusement and distraction. . . . (*LA*, 36)

Sarah Brown is alone in life and disinclined to make an effort to alter her situation. She is by choice, and apparently permanently, isolated.

This third novel is about isolation, but not all the isolation is voluntary and not all the isolation is permanent. Lady Arabel Higgins, a woman yearning for a conventional life, finds herself with a husband she is unable to understand and a son whose peculiarities she refuses to acknowledge. Her husband is so foreign to her that it is never clear whether he is still living or dead. Her son Richard is a wizard. Wanting an ordinary son, she simply ignores all his strange powers and pretends that his behavior is perfectly normal. Longing for the commonplace, she is hampered by the magic in the world around her. Refusing to accept the inconceivable, she is isolated from the reality of her family. Imprisoned by her own determination to be conventional, she consciously rejects what she knows to be true. Before the novel ends there is a suggestion that Lady Arabel may find some comfort in her isolation; she may welcome her son's child even though the mother is clearly not from the appropriate social stratum.

Richard's true love (he never seems to have gotten around to marrying her), Peony, is a battered weed of a woman, unlovely by conventional standards. When she finally abandons herself to magic she becomes the true love of Richard the wizard and the mother-to-be of her longtime child-companion "Elbert." A most unromantic character, Peony is gloriously aware of the beauty of the sky above her in spite of the grime and despair of the world around her. Before meeting Albert, Peony hated everyone and everything. "It seemed like people was all rotten, an' as if all the churches an' all the cherities was the rottenest of all the lot. Well, then dearie, Elbert blew in" (*LA*, 63). Yet even Peony, when she realized the extra-human quality of her only friend, the child Albert, was frightened and tried to run away from him. Albert found her and led her to a train, where she met Richard the wizard. During the ten days of his leave from the war, he fathers the child she is expecting in the middle of May. Peony, whose sordid life was transformed by the magic of Albert, "was not in her first youth, in fact she was comfortably into her second. Her voice was so beautiful that it almost made one shy, but her choice of language, tending as it did in the other direction, reassured one. . . . On the whole, she looked like the duckling of the story, serenely conscious of a secret swanhood" (*LA*, 60—61). Peony transcends the grime of poverty, her identity "Tonk: unmarried wife" on the card in the Charity Society file, and enters a world of witches, wizards, and everlasting boys. The inconceivable is her salvation.

Lady Arabel Higgins discovers that marriage brings isolation when she realizes there is in her husband more than she can understand and there is much about her son that she does not choose to understand. Peony's experience with Richard is liberating and comforting. With no pledges made and none asked, she is quietly confident of the correctness of what she has done. But her relationship with the father of her child could hardly be considered an example of a happy marriage since they never seem to have bothered to marry. However, marriage is not dismissed in this novel as worthless. Miss Meta Motsyn Ford, an "utter Socialist," a devotee of the occult, a victim of "nerve storms," is cured of her nerve storms and presumably of her passion for socialism and the occult when she accepts the proposal, inspired by a magic powder, of a dour Mr. Tovey. Marriage seems to be what they both want, but no hint is given that this will be a marriage of passion or that the two will be close companions. There is, though, the very strong suggestion that the two will be very pleased with themselves in the expected roles of husband and wife.

Magic liberates Peony and brings about the marriage of Miss Ford. However, Sarah Brown, who accepts without wonder the presence of magic, is irrevocably isolated from shared emotion and lasting contact with other people. Nothing magic happens to the outside of Sarah Brown, but the magic of her own imagination provides dreams that compensate for, in fact eclipse, a meager external reality. Guarding her dreams and the world within her, Sarah moves through an outer world of which she will never be a part, sustained by an inner world of her own choosing.

Living Alone emphasizes the pervasiveness of isolation and establishes magic as a reality. The presence of magic, of fairies, wizards, and dragons, does not in any way detract from the seriousness of this novel. Writers as diverse as Jonathan Swift, Oscar Wilde, H. G. Wells, Jorge Luis Borges, Stanislaw Lem, Ursula K. Le Guin and Harold Bloom, to name but a very few, have all employed the "unreal" or fantastic to develop their visions of a truth. Reasonable readers are much quicker to perceive the error of excessive rationality in Houyhnhnms much admired by Gulliver than they would be to acknowledge the same error in themselves. Fantasy serves paradoxically to distance the reader from the action of the story while encouraging him to recognize the personal truth of the fantastic world. For instance, when Benson uses two witches to demonstrate the shallows of unreflecting patriotism and unexamined prejudice, the reader can see the problem more quickly because he is less personally involved with witches than with people. This same technique will be useful later in *Goodbye, Stranger* when Benson defuses resentment of her characterization of an insensitive husband by attributing his personality to the fact that he is a fairy in a man's body.

The fantasy in *Living Alone* reaffirms the idea that complete accurate communication is impossible. We see normal people failing to understand each other and their world; we also see beings with unusual abilities who are no better able to communicate than mere mortals. For example, having accidentally demolished a bird's nest while hoeing a row of beans, Sarah discovers from fairy fieldhands that a bird's trilling may be beautiful but beauty is not the emblem of joy. Thus, Shelley's blithe spirit, the skylark, may have been singing in despair. As a fairy explained it, "I don't know the actual facts of the case, but without a doubt your friend Shelley was standing on the unfortunate bird's nest all the time he was writing his poem" (*LA*, 176). The fairies themselves, with their immortal bodies but absence of soul, believe humans in pain are simply flaunting their mortal superiority. Humans, meanwhile, envy the fairies their apparent freedom from care.

Failure in communication is not caused only by misunderstood appearance. How an unfortunate dragon says what he says conveys more of his essential nature than he would like to have revealed. The unimpressive dragon's discipline problems on Higgins Farm are recognizable in his speech pattern as he tries to keep the fairy fieldhands working: "Get on with your work, you people, do. There, you see, they defy me to an extent. . . ." As the narrator points out "Directly the dragon said 'to an extent' without qualifying the extent, one saw why it had no gift of discipline" (*LA*, 168). The dragon is indecisive and insecure, the lack of force behind his words is perfectly clear. But inner conviction matching outer articulation does not assure communication either, as is demonstrated after the battle of two witches during an air raid. Although both witches superficially understand each other, they cannot finally understand how they arrived at their predicament: facing each other on a shrinking cloud while their broomsticks fight above them. Angela, the English witch, concludes "There must be some misunderstanding somewhere. Or else some real Evil somewhere." When the German witch, speaking with conviction and self-assurance, counters with, "There is,

England is Evil" (*LA*, 147), one suspects that the real evil is precisely the failure to communicate and understand themselves and each other. Neither side examines its premise or defines its terms. The penalty for the failure in understanding is death, to young men dying in trenches and to the German witch falling to her death when her side of the cloud is disintegrated, ironically, by the reverberations of the explosion of the German bombs falling on London.

Like all of Benson's novels, *Living Alone* is primarily concerned with the situation of isolated individuals. Although the chapters are given titles that seem to call attention to a pattern of organization, the reader may emerge less with a sense of having read a well-designed novel than with the feeling of having completed a collection of loosely connected short stories. In spite of this weakness in structure, the novel achieves a telling effect through the ambivalence with which it leaves the reader at its conclusion. In tension with the conventional pity for Sarah Brown, deaf and alone in a strange land, is an almost resentful recognition that Sarah Brown does not need anyone's pity: she manages quite well alone and prefers not to be bothered even by well-intentioned concern.

Recognizing the inadequacy of rationality as a means of coping with an incomprehensible and seemingly indifferent universe, Stella Benson's first three novels assert an extra-reality and defend the necessity for individuality even if a unique identity ensures isolation. These works are fundamentally concerned with depreciating the immediacy of observable external reality. Yet they are not simple fantasies. While encouraging fantasy as an escape, these novels not only have an anti-convention bias which often characterizes the outlook of the young, but also recognize human fallibility with a compassion found in the mature.

Chapter Five
Living in the Real World

Stella Benson's last four completed novels[1] focus not on alternative realities, nor on the inner life at odds with outer activities, but on the nature of individual reality. The novels reflect a sensibility finely attuned to the human weaknesses that contribute to individual unhappiness. Benson herself was not unfamiliar with unhappiness during this time: her fourth novel, *The Poor Man*, was begun in the aftermath of a California sojourn that had been emotionally exhausting, and the last three novels were written while she lived what she believed to be an intellectually barren life in China. In 1924, the year *Pipers and a Dancer* was published, Benson admitted, "I seem to have become so well-rooted now in domestic China small-port life that anything written about the old Stella Benson who use [*sic*] to walk the world in a constant state of excitement and defensive illusionment seems to me now to be written about a remote and unknown person. However, perhaps the present state is another form of defense."[2] She never seemed able to defend herself completely against feelings of inadequacy and loneliness, but her novels reveal an increasing inclination to search for the possible and positive in human relations and to de-romanticize loneliness.

The Poor Man

The Poor Man marks an important change in Benson's art. The earlier novels give the reader the feeling that he is being included in the world of a witty and determinedly hopeful narrator. The narrator's observations have assumed a common disinclination on the part of the reader to bow to an external reality. And the reader gets caught up in that assumption. The fact that none of the early novels end on a note of resounding optimism paradoxically encourages the acceptance of the ideals of the narrator because there is no simple assertion that these ideals will ever truly prevail in the world. The omniscient narrator in *The Poor Man*, on the other hand, does not include the reader in a comfortable spectator's box with a reassuring voice reminding him that the world needn't really be as bad as all that. Twelve years after writing it, Benson said, "*The Poor Man* was written in a mood of revulsion against visions . . . tremblings and hesitancies now are induced by bogeys more nearly real and more difficult to placate. The approach to *The Poor Man* himself, I think, was the first admission on my part of a principle that now seems important to me—the refusal to imply an ought or an ought not . . . the withholding of comment."[3] Nonetheless, while allowing the reader to draw his own conclusions from the facts presented, the narrator conveys the facts with gentle irony and compassionate understanding.

The poor man is Edward R. Williams, a partially deaf young Englishman who has been in San Francisco long enough to have driven his most sympathetic California acquaintance to resort to a transparent subterfuge to send him to China. The plan fails when Edward meets Emily, an attractive young Englishwoman, and forces himself into a party travelling with her to Yosemite. The group consists of eight people: four American and four English. The Americans are Rhoda Romero and her ex-husband Avery Bird, the divorced Mrs. Melsie Ponting, and a harmless man-about-town, Banner Hope. Edward, Emily, the handsome self-centered journalist Tam McTab, and his wife Lucy are the British contingent. Before the trip is brought to its unpleasant end, it becomes quite obvious that Emily is in love with Tam McTab and that Edward is, as he tells himself, "deafly and drunkenly and neurotically" in love with Emily. Unfortunately, Edward brings the trip to a disastrous end by having to be driven, crying, to a hospital for relief from a sinus infection. While he is in the hospital Emily and the McTabs leave for China, accompanied by Stone Ponting, a boy being sent by his mother to live with his businessman father in China. Once out of the hospital, Edward tries to raise money to pursue Emily. His unsuccessful career as a book salesman ends as he uses a borrowed bicycle as collateral for a loan to buy a drink.

Edward finally gets money for his passage to China by accepting money offered by Avery Bird who is desperate to get rid of him. Unable to find Emily in Hong Kong, Edward continues to Peking. There he discovers Stone Ponting alone, fortified against the world's indifference by a thousand dollars sent him by his father who is away on business. Emily and the McTabs left several weeks earlier. Edward ingratiates himself with the boy, borrows money from him to buy a new suit, and convinces him that they should go in search of Emily. With Edward looking like "an unsuccessful dentist" in his new suit, the two travellers find Tam and Lucy in Chungking, but discover Emily has left—thrown out by Lucy when Emily succumbed to heat and unhappiness and tried to claim Tam as her own. Emily has gone to Shanghai, so Edward and Stone leave for Shanghai.

While Stone is at a movie in Shanghai, Edward takes most of what is left of Stone's thousand dollars and goes in search of Emily. He finds her, dines with her alone in her hotel room, believes that he is going to spend the night with her, and finally faces total rejection from the woman he has followed for thousands of miles. She cries "I can't bear you. I couldn't bear to touch you—you poor sickly thing. . . ."[4]

Although before its publication Benson admitted she was not certain of her book's reception in America, she was not prepared for the storm of protest which arose when her American friends read it. Even her closest California friends were upset. The furor was primarily inspired by Benson's merciless satire of the "hundred-per-center" type of American, a type scathingly exposed in the Weber family.

The American of the Weber type chooses many of his words for their potential catch in the throat, as it were. *Motherhood, manhood, lovelight, grip-'o-the-hand*, the movies have made words of this kind music in the American ear. But words with home in them are the most popular—homestead, homeland, home-site, home-town, home-builder. . . . We who live in houses and can see the word Mother in print with dry eyes or hear the glugging of someone else's baby over its food in a cafeteria without vicarious domestic ecstasy, must seem very coarse to Americans. (*PM*, 131)

Mamie Weber, who selects her beaux in a rather indiscriminate way (any available male is suitable), her rude brother Cliff, her taciturn father, and her shrill laughing mother seem to embody all that could be coarse and insensitive without being consciously malicious. Mamie's father has one conversation with Edward:

"Well, young feller, how much better d'you like this country than yer own?"

"No better," replied Edward nervously. He hastened to add apologetically, "You see, I have an affection for England because it's my home—I mean my Homeland, as it were. Just the same as you'd like America best even if you came to England—"

Mr. Weber laughed and set his toothpick to work on a rather inaccessible tooth. "Reckon I shouldn't think anything of England," he said in a final voice.

"Well, that's what I mean," said Edward, growing rather red. "That's rather what I feel about America when you compare it with England."

Pop leaned forward and levelled his toothpick at Edward's face. "Now, see here, Son," he said, showing only two of his left-hand teeth.

Miss Weber shrieked, "Aw, cut it out, Pop—and you forget it too, Ed. Pop's a reg'lar whizz at politics." (*PM*, 132–33)

The Webers are rude, ignorant, stupid people but they are not deliberately cruel. They are incapable of introspection and equally incapable of evaluating an external reality. They simply accept the clichés and the standard, conventional responses as the only ones possible. When embraced with such unreflecting passivity any ideal emotion must become sentimental.

This novel is an early salvo in Benson's continuing battle against what she saw as leveling mediocrity and crass commercialism breeding out from the United States. She spent a lifetime decrying the sentimentality and the mindless acceptance of clichés, slogans, and advertisements that she believed characteristic of many Americans. Several of her short stories focus specifically on this theme. But the main business of *The Poor Man* is not to vent anti-American prejudice; the novel has broader aims. It remorselessly strips the defensive facade from imperfect humans and reveals the wretchedness within. In their bigotry and ignorance the Webers seem quite content. Afflicted with a different type of selfishness, it is the introspective characters in the novel who are far from happy.

The Poor Man directs the reader's attention to a reality that is almost totally devoid of romance—of beautiful passion inspiring sentimental sighs from the reader. The night Edward R. Williams meets his countrywoman Emily he twice announces his love for her. The situation is not a sentimental one: Edward is too drunk to order dinner and Emily dances with a man who throws a hotel matchbox at her. While Emily dances, Edward is relieved because he has to make no social effort and need not fear being laughed at. Yet the reader may begin to believe that Edward's love for Emily may be his salvation. The fact that Edward recognizes that Emily talks too much could be a sign that he can cope with reality and only needs another's support to bolster his confidence. With love he might be transformed into a more positive and admirable member of society. However, that sentimental hope is dampened when the narrator observes that "Emily was always affected by the skins and shapes of men and women. The last hour had been made almost unbearable to her by the fact that Edward had red spots all over his forehead and chin" (*PM*, 31). Edward, however, was for once unconscious of his skin affliction: "He really forgot that Emily could see him; he knew only that he could see Emily. If he were in a book, he thought, the spots would not be mentioned. If the book were well written the reader would now be saying, 'Our Hero is surely more in love than ever man was before'"

(*PM*, 31). Faced with this sentimental overstatement, the reader should be warned to examine critically the traditional sentimental response to hints of romance. What sort of love is Edward capable of? How would his love be defined? And what of Emily? Perhaps the only honest thing she has said during the evening is, "You don't know me. You only know what I look like. You have heard nothing but lies from me. I have only room for one true thing in my life" (*PM*, 31). What she seems to have meant by the "one true thing" was her love for Tam McTab, the married journalist for whom she works, but long before the end of the novel the one true thing in Emily is recognized as her determination to see herself clearly.

Emily, single and supporting herself, is like all of the women in the novel, quite able to fend for herself. In love with a vain and weak man, she has maintained outward decorum over a period of several years. Lucy, the wife of the man Emily loves, seems to be the stereotypical woman and wife: passive and self-effacing. Yet Benson demonstrates the strength that can lie hidden behind such a submissive exterior; it is Lucy's conscious and determined wifely devotion that enables her to triumph over her rival. Waiting for her opportunity to get rid of Emily, she has only to continue to be the admiring, uncritical audience for her husband to ensure his continued dependence upon her. Rhoda Romero, political activist and devoted bohemian, is loyal to and motherly toward her ex-husband. Melsie Ponting, seeking reassurance through evidence of her sexual attractiveness, is a pitiful woman doomed to loneliness and disappointment, but her selfishness gives her the strength to reject her maternal responsibilities in order to retain her self-image of young beauty. She is certainly not to be admired for her neglect of her son, but she does make decisions about her life and then acts upon these decisions. Even Mamie Weber, realizing her identity will be derived from her relationship with men, chooses not to wait passively to be found by eligible young men, but pursues them actively. None of these women, with the possible exception of Rhoda Romero, is portrayed as particularly admirable; furthermore, none of them awakens deep sympathy in the reader. Benson is careful to modulate their pathos with farce; they are more ridiculous than tragic. Yet for all that, they are portrayed more positively than the men.

All of the men appear to be essentially helpless: Avery Bird is distraught when separated from his ex-wife; Banner Hope shies away from any hint of close contact with another human, as though afraid to expose himself to rebuff; and Tam McTab, the famous journalist, is absolutely dependent upon the constant stroking and ego-inflation offered by his wife. Edward Williams seems to be the strongest of the men, although he is incapable of, or has decided against, any effort that would bring him closer to what he considers to be a more heroic posture. And yet his determination to enjoy his misery is in a sense a positive stand.

Edward, like Emily, is introspective, but his masochistic enjoyment of his misery is all his own. He is a person who "looked forward almost eagerly to atrocious pain forever" (*PM*, 93), and he seems to be a man likely to realize his desire. Physically unattractive, socially inept, personally contemptible, he contains characteristics of the gardener in *I Pose*, Jay in *This Is The End*, and Sarah Brown in *Living Alone*, all presented in the worst possible light. Edward imagines himself in various poses, even mentally casts himself in the role of a hero, but because "he was in the habit of refuting morbidly every statement he himself made" (*PM*, 9), he bitterly castigates himself for his attempt to improve his self-image through fantasizing: "I am defective. Our hero in a tragic mood of self-realisation. Our Hero indeed! I am not even my own hero" (*PM*, 88). This self-contempt is accompanied by no salutary effort to improve himself.

Yet Edward is not without some merit. With characteristic Bensonian irony, the narrator explains "Music to Edward Williams had no connection with words or rules or understanding. He could not have been at all musical. . . . Music to him was always anticipation, even when it was over," and it could make him "blind with delight for several seconds." Thus, far from not being at all musical, partially deaf Edward appreciates music as music, not as a source of inspiration for clever epigrams: "he never thought of saying: 'you know Scriabin is clean, my dear, clean like a scrubbed olive,' or 'It has been wittily said that Moussorgski is the spiritual son of Ouida and Charlemagne,' or any of the things sounding rather like that, that we expect to hear from musical people as the Victrola falls silent" (*PM*, 10). Edward's unaffected appreciation of sound is not always marred by his deafness. In fact, his deafness becomes, in some respects, an asset. After a piece of music ended,

> A woman's sharp voice said, "Well say, listen, what was that? It was a dandy piece," and Edward heard the man with a cocktail shaker between his knees reply, "That was the song of the twelve eagles after the emeralds of the South Sea lost their fragrance." Someone added, "They were crushed the day the love-tinker died on a hill of violets in Vienna." Edward Williams was pleased with this conversation, although, of course, he knew that it had not taken place. He knew well that he was more than half deaf, and in many moods he welcomed the insight that his infirmity gave him into matters that did not exist. His two

friends had been telling each other facts that both knew and that Edward did not wish to know. Neither would, of course, dream of mentioning emeralds or hills of violets except when it was really necessary and helpful to do so. Edward did not care. He felt that his mind's eye had acquired one picture the more without the trouble of acquiring a fact. (*PM*, 11).

Even without the background of the first three Benson novels, the reader must recognize that the response Edward imagines to the shrill request for a piece of identifying fact is more lovely, and more appreciative of the beauty of the music, than its official name could ever be. With the memory of Sarah Brown's lonely external existence in *Living Alone* compensated for by the world of her imagination, of the Secret Worlds in *This Is The End* which comforted the inhabitants of a cold reality, the reader might begin to believe that Edward R. Williams will be like Jay, unhappy with the world around him and retreating into his secret world. But Edward never escapes from the world and never really tries to. He enjoys his misery and profits from his weaknesses.

Although Edward is absolutely servile, he is not totally insensitive. This novel demonstrates Benson's skill in characterization: allowing Edward the insight to see himself as others see him, Benson risks creating strong sympathy for him in the reader. She adds to the danger by allowing Edward spontaneous and unpretentious appreciation of music. Yet his few good points serve not to elevate the reader's opinion of him, but rather to reduce sympathy for a man who apparently could be a better person if he chose.

Determined that the reader should not believe Edward a wretched man with hidden nobility, Benson emphasizes Edward's complete absence of conventional scruples. "He had no shame about accepting money. He lacked manly pride. If Melsie Ponting had offered him money he would have taken it gladly. He would have pretended to himself that it was a great struggle and great humiliation to accept money but really he would have been delighted. . . . One thing Edward was not too proud but too shy to do. He could not actually ask for money" (*PM*, 114–15). However, he had no compunction about simply taking money. With no remorse he left a friendless child destitute in Shanghai: "Somehow if he never saw Stone again Edward felt that the money would not matter. If one were never reminded one need not remember. A crime of which one was never accused was no crime. Edward had no self-accuser on the subject of money. There were limits to his humility and to his humiliation" (*PM*, 233–34). But the limits were few. The straw of self-justification not seriously grasped before he sold Cliff Weber's bicycle for a drink and fare to San Francisco was: "Cliff said I'd probably skip with it so he won't be surprised. . . . Nor will Pop. Pop will say, 'That's what comes of picking up with a Britisher.' He'll spit and pretend he's spitting on England" (*PM*, 147−48). Edward's self-justification may contain an accurate forecast of the Webers' reactions, but the fact remains he did in effect steal the bicycle. The Webers are unpleasant people but they have been treated shabbily by Edward. However, Edward was not troubled by the subtle moral distinctions: "Edward had not only no objection to telling lies, he even failed as a rule to notice how broadly he lied" (*PM*, 171).

Edward's failure to be concerned with preserving truth is not unique in the novel. In fact, truth itself becomes almost impossible to define. The nebulous nature of truth is demonstrated by the responses to Emily's spontaneous proposal that everyone "pose as being absolutely honest." The group around the campfire obliges, and their admissions about their lies are revealing both for clarifying the type of people they are and for emphasizing the illusive nature of truth. Like T. S. Eliot's Prufrock, the characters in this novel prepare faces to meet faces: masks and poses are the realities of their lives.

The first to respond to Emily's suggestion is Tam's wife Lucy:

"Why Emily, don't talk like that. I try not to lie at all, of course."

"Oh, I try frightfully hard to lie," said Tam. "I am always deeply disappointed if I don't succeed in deceiving everyone I know about what I am and what I have whenever I want to."

"Oh, you naughty, naughty man!" said Melsie Ponting. "As for me, I only lie to make a funny yarn funnier. I never mean to deceive a fly."

"I lie," said Edward, "to save myself from myself." He thought this sounded modest and tragic.

"I lie when I am angry or when I am frightened," said Rhoda. "If I were always calm I should never lie at all, I guess. Except that I never tell anything that happened to me exactly the way it happened."

"I have no conscience at all," Banner Hope said. "I remember when my Momma used to catch me stealing the candies. . . . "

"Truth," announced Avery Bird, "is a bastard begotten by a steam-locomotive and born of the scent of jasmine—if you get me. Truth is the ghost of a decadent vice, clanking steel chains: Mary Magdalene was crucified on truth instead of a wooden cross—"

"Oh, for the land's sake, Avery," explained Rhoda. "Do you have to act so damned complex? Nobody gets you, believe me. It's because he's a Jew. . . . " she added apologetically to the others as she took Avery's hand.

"I think you're all posing," said Emily. Her clenched hands became slack as though with disappointment. "If I began to say how much I lied I should pose as a miserable sinner. Yet I do lie, to save myself from the anger—which I deserve—of other people. And I lie often in order to seem uniquely honest. Oh, hang it all, there's no getting away from pose after all. We're all posing as liars now because it's more popular and funny to be liars—"

"Lucy didn't," said Tam as though Lucy were his property. (*PM*, 82–84)

This series of statements reveals both Benson's technique and the theme of the novel. Whereas in earlier works Benson would have evaluated these comments for the reader, now she records them and continues the narrative. With the decision to record rather than to report and comment, Benson gave larger scope to her very acute ability to render dialogue. As she was well aware, words may convey much more than their intended explicit meaning. The decision to record also, of course, demands more from the reader, as *The Poor Man* reinforces once again Benson's insistence that literal accuracy and rationality are not synonymous with truth. In the passage quoted above, everyone pretends to honesty by admitting to lies, but the admissions are often deceptive, or outright falsehoods. Paradoxically, the lies about when they lie often disclose more truth than attempts at honest self-appraisal might. For instance, the first person to respond, Lucy, is a woman who says she tries not to lie at all. In one sense what she is saying is true, but on another level what she is saying is completely false.

Lucy's strong sense of propriety may indeed restrain her from making verbal assertions that are demonstrably contrary to observable fact. However, this same sense of propriety demands that she nurture a determined blindness to her surroundings. In the midst of a forest she tries to surround herself with drawing-room small talk. In spite of the fact that Emily made no great effort to hide her feelings for Tam, Lucy's external demeanor during the three years that Emily has been Tam's secretary has not once revealed a jealous wife beneath. Yet, as Tam admits, when Emily began her scene, when she declared her love for Tam in a manner that was unmistakable, it was as though Lucy had been waiting for this very moment. Moving swiftly, she packed Emily's things and put them and Emily out of the house. Avoiding lies as lies are usually defined, Lucy seems to live a lie in her determined oblivion. Yet her apparent pretense that she has no competition for Tam reflects an accurate assessment of the reality of her marriage. She is safe, admiring, and tolerant; the egocentric Tam could not afford the uncertainty of life with a person determined to assert herself as a person, a person who would not always be mutely admiring. So Emily, who could disconcert Tam, never had a chance of marrying him. Lucy's actions belie her recognition of Tam's interest in Emily, but the pretense itself inspires the reality she insists upon.

Tam's statement about his lying is not precisely accurate either. The object of his endeavor is never simply to lie, nor is his disappointment the result of failing to deceive; Tam's objective is to preen himself constantly, and his disappointment arises when he finds that he is not the center of attention. He may lie to gain attention and be disappointed when he fails to secure the interest that he seeks, but the lying itself is the means to his end and not, as his assertion implies, the end itself. His objective is not bald deceit, although deceit may be involved in securing the admiration of those around him.

Melsie Ponting, whose stock of funny yarns is conspicuous in its absence, does not lie to entertain others. She is too self-absorbed to be seriously conscious of the needs of other people. "Mrs. Ponting lived entirely from her own point of view. This was her life, to charm those whom she needed, to wound those who rebuffed her, to ignore those with whom she was acquainted. Her imagination was completely blind and deaf; wounds or joys outside of herself were inconceivable to her" (*PM*, 114). Melsie does not try to deceive other people; she tries to construct a pleasant world for herself. This woman, leaving youth behind, enters loveless liaisons with undergraduates to reinforce her own belief that she can be and is an eternal nymph. The motive for Melsie's deceit is not entertainment but self-preservation.

Edward's response certainly does, as he hopes, sound modest and tragic, but it also is not quite accurate. Edward does not save himself from himself, and he does not really try to. He thinks that what he has just said, "I lie to save myself from myself," sounds modest and tragic. He does not for a moment believe he is himself either appealingly modest or compellingly tragic. Thus his lies are not lies at all; they are games he plays with himself. He is in fact excruciatingly honest in his self-appraisals.

Rhoda's statement that she only lies when she is angry or frightened is made against the background of the reader's introduction to her: she was discussing with Banner Hope her ruse for getting Edward out of the country. Rhoda, the one character in *The Poor Man* who displays compassion for others, comes closest to being honest about her lies. The equivocal "I guess" following, "If I were calm I should never lie at all," suggests a candor which enhances her image as an honest person. Yet her last statement, "Except that I never tell anything that happened to me exactly the way it happened," admits a factual distortion in every report she makes.

Banner Hope's announcement that he has no conscience is revealed, by his choice of subject for his example, to be wishful thinking. This man who "would have liked to be known as the wickedest man in San Francisco" (*PM*, 14) is no more than a good-natured, unimaginative, devotee of cocktails who must dredge up cookie-stealing from his childhood to illustrate his amorality.

Finally, Avery Bird defines truth in grandiloquent metaphorical terms and sounds ridiculous. But preposterous as his definitions are, they come closer to an appreciation of truth than the others' admissions do to honesty. His definitions also serve to prepare the reader for Emily's admissions that, in addition to using lies to save herself from the anger of other people, she also lies in order to seem uniquely honest. The reality that the very antithesis of honesty can produce the illusion of extreme honesty emphasizes the impracticality of reliance on observed reality to establish truth.

Benson once told an American friend, "I meant the character of Edward to be an absolutely servile and ignoble character treated with understanding."[5] Edward, Emily, all the characters in the novel are treated with understanding. It is a measure of Benson's success that after realizing Edward has lost Emily forever, the reader feels relief that Emily does not burden herself with such a spineless creature as Edward, sorrow that Edward must face without illusion the fact that he is as contemptible to Emily as he has imagined himself at his most despondent moments, and a certain practical satisfaction that Edward will be as unhappy as he has always wanted to be. *The Poor Man* lays bare the pitiful ploys Edward encourages in himself to maintain some sort of self-appreciation. He seldom succeeds even in eliciting pity, but he does seem to have adjusted to failure. In his apparently pointless misery he accepts his life and morbidly appreciates its deficiencies.

Pipers and a Dancer

Pipers and a Dancer was written after Benson had suffered the criticism of her California friends for her unflattering picture of Californians in *The Poor Man* and after she had come to realize how devastatingly arid life could be even in a physically beautiful setting. She began her married life in Mengtsz, China, and her letters written during the time spent there reflect a total disenchantment with her few European neighbors and an increasing tendency to question her own personal worth. Writing to Sidney Schiff, Benson explained, "every time I ride out, my eyes are perfectly happy. But I am too Ipsie-ish to live serenely with mean and spiteful neighbors."⁶ So she occupied her time with the writing of this fifth novel, the main character of which is Ipsie Wilson.

Ipsie (Mary Hippolyta Wilson) is a young Englishwoman travelling to China to marry Jacob Heming, a man she does not pretend to love. A mild shipboard flirtation with an American, Rodd Innes, wanes after a few days in the face of her torrent of self-revelations. This compulsion to explain herself does not blind her to the fact of its existence, nor does it render her imperceptive about other people. In fact, she is acutely conscious of other people: Ipsie feels her life is directed by her Showman, whose objective is to exhibit her before "a ghostly and ideal public."

When the ship reaches Hong Kong Ipsie is met by her fiancé's sister, Pauline Heming, and by Sophie Hinds who is Pauline's constant companion and who "obviously adored Pauline." While waiting in Hong Kong with Pauline for Jacob to arrive from Yueh Lai Chou, Ipsie makes it clear that she is not captivated by Pauline. Pauline's response is to dislike Ipsie and at the same time to attempt to win her over. In the meantime, Rodd Innes, who is to assume Jacob Heming's job, travels to Yueh Lai Chou and discovers Heming to be a miserable, thoroughly disliked, narrow-minded, bitter man. Rodd determines to warn Ipsie not to marry Jacob, but before he can act Jacob is kidnapped by a band of Chinese brigands. Rodd telegrams the news to Pauline and Ipsie and tries to initiate a rescue mission. Heming, however, has so antagonized everyone that his fate is at best a matter of indifference to his neighbors, and seems to be a source of pleasure for the Chinese magistrate who has been repeatedly insulted by Heming.

When Ipsie, Pauline, and Sophie Hinds arrive in Yueh Lai Chou to await Jacob's return, Rodd, whose interest in Ipsie is rekindled, competes with Pauline for control of Ipsie. During a celebration following news that Heming's release has been arranged, it seems that Rodd has won the contest. Ipsie drinks some champagne and then announces that she is not going to marry Jacob after all. She goes on to say that she is not going to marry ever but intends to have as many lovers as she can. Here Rodd interrupts her, saying that she has gone too far and that he intends to marry her. Before the matter is settled Pauline whisks Ipsie off to bed, claiming that Ipsie has not really recovered from the infection in her lungs which struck her when she first arrived in Yueh Lai Chou.

The ensuing days are extremely unpleasant for Ipsie. Pauline, perceiving that smothering Ipsie in kindness has not won her, attacks with the cold shell of anger. With Ipsie disturbed because she is ignored by Pauline, word arrives that Jacob is ill and resting ten hours away.

Pauline accompanies the soldiers who are going to take him provisions and escort him home, and an hour after Pauline's departure Ipsie, believing Jacob is dying, decides to go and comfort him and so begin to construct a satisfying memory. In fact, at the very moment Ipsie is convincing herself that Jacob is thinking longingly of her, he is feverishly comparing her contemptuously to a Panamanian prostitute whom he had loved and by whom he had been deserted.

Before the party arrives the hapless Jacob is dead, and so is transformed into a perfect memory. At that point "Rodd, it seemed, was dead and Jacob victoriously alive."[7] Rodd tries to focus Ipsie's attention on himself, but loses her finally when Pauline's veneer of efficiency cracks and Ipsie's Showman finds another Ipsie to display—"One who brings Comfort to the Weak and Sorrowful." Instead of joining Rodd, Ipsie decides to live in Arizona with Pauline.

The reviewer in the London *Times* gave a succinct summary of what Ipsie-ish people are like. They are "distracted between that which they wish to be, that which they are, that which they think they are, that which the presence of other people makes them; and each of these parts is in turn distracted by its own multiplicity." He goes on to assert,

> It is all good and true, and Miss Benson's quickness is kept on the stretch by the girl's confusion within, but there is not room enough, as we said, nor time enough allowed for the girl to bring her scattered selves together and be seen for what she is, one young woman. . . . It is quite different with the rest [of the characters], for they are seized from without and need only to be seen as they affect the girl . . . these are very shrewdly understood . . . [Benson] riddles them with a phrase. She is so quick and so sharp that she gets her phrase home nearly always; it is nearly always the right stroke, hitting the right point.[8]

This reviewer would probably have thought that Benson's biographer Ellis Roberts was on the right track when he said that although "It is not a question of the strangeness, the abnormality, the excessive unlikeness of any character [Ipsie] is the least coherent of Stella's women: for in writing of her Stella loaded Ipsie with too many of her own moods, too much of her own mental distress, and also gives her certain characteristics which were Stella's but would never have been Ipsie's."[9] The logic of his assessment is a bit vague, but he seems to believe he is criticizing the execution of the vision of the novel, when in fact he may be unhappy with the vision itself.

With *Pipers and a Dancer* Benson makes some interesting changes in the standard formula for women in novels. Unmarried women were supposed to be dissatisfied with their husbandless condition. When occasionally the reader ran across a woman not pining for a husband, the woman was usually strident, abrasive, and generally unpleasant—and of course somehow corrupt because content with the company of women. Women who did not consider marriage their life's goal had been easily dismissed from much literature by the suggestions that if they were not being punished for past indiscretions, for too much love of men, they were lesbians. The hints of lesbianism in novels with independent female characters were of varying intensity, but nonetheless it was often clear that a woman's political and economic theories were aberrant because her sexual preferences were also. When young girls were attracted to these women (usually caught up in their political rhetoric), if the girl was the heroine she would almost inevitably reject her activist, dangerous female friend and accept a conventional proposal from a male suitor. A well-known example can be found in Henry James's *The Bostonians*. The feminist Olive Chancellor loses her influence over the younger woman Verena Tarrant and is supplanted by Basil Ransom.

Benson's young heroine is not deflected from the embrace of an aggressive female; she welcomes the alliance for the range of experience it offers her. Furthermore, her fragmented personality characterized by the feeling that her essential identity was lost at birth is caused not by an absence of identity but by a rejection of an identity that is socially unacceptable and biologically impossible. The diminutive Ipsie seeking safety as Mrs. Jacob Heming recognizes perfection in the idea of her dead brother Conrad. In fact, there are in each of her moods and poses slight impersonations of specific traits of her three dead brothers. Unable to live her masculine identity, she is driven by it (her Show*man*) to reflect the expectations of others.

As the novel opens, Ipsie seems destined to have to choose, and the choice initially seems to be between her miserable fiancé Jacob and the pleasant Rodd Innes.

Jacob Heming is a man as morbid as Edward R. Williams, but in his misery he inspires a pity in the reader that Edward did not receive. The pity arises in part from the realization that although Jacob is justly disliked he, unlike Edward, does not understand that he is contemptible.

> Nothing was right in his eyes. His eyes and his heart were haunted by the ghosts of wrongs and slights, of threats and impossibilities. . . . Ipsie haunted him more kindly than did most of the more virile ghosts. For this reason Heming

thought very little of Ipsie. She was a good homely little body and he had no doubt that she would, when properly trained, make a good little wife. In his own eyes he was a mild and unpretentious man and his ideas of marriage were utterly unpretentious. . . . Heming honestly reviewed his own character again, seeking some explanation of the behaviour of the French neighbours towards him—some explanation of the behaviour of God towards him. He seemed to himself to be an excellent fellow, only too ready to take his part in any clean fun, a ladies' man, no vices. There was, he felt, nothing to dislike in him. All the neighbours at Yueh Lai Chou were, he was convinced, his inferiors, mentally, morally and physically—especially the French. (*PD*, 66, 67, 71)

Fat, forty, and a social failure, Jacob is depending on Ipsie to give stability, normalcy, and a sense of belonging to his life. His expectation is not that "wee Mary" (his name for Ipsie) as a person will be a comfort to the person that he is, but that the acquisition of a wife will bring him pleasure and probably (although he does not specifically articulate this idea) integrate him into a more acceptable social life. At the very least the two of them will enjoy the "cinema palaces" of Shanghai, and he will take pleasure in possessing a wife who brings order and cleanliness to his house.

Jacob is not, however, simply a pathetic man. Being self-centered and imperceptive, he is also potentially cruel in his blind determination to see only the woman he wants to see in his wife. He does, of course, believe that women are made for marriage. Thus, in his opinion his sister was ruined by her education: "All that education unsettles a woman—prevented Pauline marrying, I always say" (*PD*, 36). His ideal woman is a Panamanian prostitute whose only fancy was for a fancy man, whose only concern was to please men—that was the proper concern of all women. Ipsie unfortunately "had fancies that seemed deliberately queer, . . . [but] she would end by understanding what a man wanted of a woman, of that he felt sure. Marriage taught even fanciful women that" (*PD*, 131). His less brutal expression of this idea is to dismiss her art out of hand: "Her drawing is a nice quiet amusement for her, but she hasn't got any real talent. . . . Women soon give up these fal-lals once they're married" (*PD*, 42, 37).

Ipsie, who is haunted by an elusive ghost of some lost self, travels to China seeking in Jacob a security, an anchor for her identity. She is not really expecting love but hopes for self-knowledge. "Ipsie had known Jacob, it seemed to her, well. She had known at least what to expect of him. An incurious safe person standing on firm ground, a person who would hold her hand and steady her on the slippery giddy peak that was herself" (*PD*, 85). However, when she receives Jacob's letter of welcome to Hong Kong addressed to "My own wee Mary," Ipsie recognizes beyond doubt that the Ipsie who is a creature of moods does not and will not exist for Jacob Heming:

"It's a great mistake, but the great mistakes pass—only little things live and last. I shall be an anchored woman called Mrs. Jacob Heming; I shall have a neat store-room; I shall have babies; I shall not die alone." . . . Ipsie wanted to be saved from Ipsie and yet she could not bear her secret Ipsie to die. Wee Mary would be a poor exhibition for the Showman. Wee Mary was blind to terror and delight. Wee Mary had never known Conrad.
"I shall have *Sic transit gloria mundi* engraved inside my wedding-ring." (*PD*, 56, 85)

Ipsie clearly considers marriage the death of the spirit, but this restriction that kills can also be a prison that imposes calm and order. Restricted to one role, she may find peace.

Although she does not look forward with pleasure to life with Jacob, Ipsie is for quite a while prepared to submit to his vision of her in order to establish a coherent identity. Yet that identity is so alien to her hidden core that she finally does reject it. In fact, she does not simply reject Jacob's vision of her, she rejects the role of wife. Announcing that she will not marry Jacob, Ipsie continues, "I will not marry anyone. I'm not faithful enough. I'll just have as many lovers as I can" (*PD*, 142). Taking this stand, she is moving closer to a more masculine identity. Men may take lovers with impunity, women may not. But Ipsie has distinctly unfeminine attitudes toward love. "For real women love was the tree on which the fruit of life was hung; for Ipsie love was a spray of peach-blossoms in a fine wind" (*PD*, 119). Were she a man, this definition of love would cause no comment, but this young woman violates the time-honored convention paraphrased by Lord Byron from Mme de Staël's *De l'influence des passions* (1796): "Man's love is of a man's life a thing apart, / 'Tis woman's whole existence." Not Rodd or Jacob but Ipsie looks forward to falling in love and growing out of love within a week: here is a distinctly unfeminine attitude.

Rodd is relieved by Ipsie's decision not to marry Jacob; he balks at her decision to take lovers. Refusing to be her first lover, he insists that they marry. Rodd's several virtues certainly make him seem an acceptable suitor. He is quite conventional and naturally socially successful. He also has an unchecked ability to empathize with others: he is the only person in Yueh Lai Chou to be filled with pity as well as distaste for Jacob. All of Jacob's neighbors dislike him so much that they can avert their eyes from the misery that haunts the bigoted, stupid man; Rodd cannot. Furthermore, Rodd recognizes the chameleon character of Ipsie: "She had seemed to him a precarious performer in the world's circus, tremulously balanced on a very thin wire" (PD, 27). Although he begins to understand her, Rodd continues to search for a hidden core of identity. He refuses to dictate what that identity must be.

Rodd, who could adapt himself to be charming, especially to people he did not care about, was remarkably like Ipsie, who would become the Ipsie she believed other people wanted to see. The major difference between them was that Ipsie and her Showman tried too hard, covered the fundamental unease in any pose with chatter, and occasionally misread the cue. Rodd, on the other hand, instinctively did the right thing. This difference might well be attributed to Rodd's comfort with his roles and to Ipsie's discomfort because her roles were all those expected of a woman. The role of woman did not come naturally to her.

Rodd's vision of Ipsie is radically different from Jacob's or Pauline's. He is fascinated by his image of the girl and attracted to the mystery of the girl rather than in love with the human being before him. In fact, what he feels seems to be an admirable impulse to protect her and encourage her buried single identity to flower. What he does not understand is that Ipsie is not seeking to develop her personally discovered essential identity, but rather is seeking help in sustaining one acceptable identity or series of poses to which she may return with some regularity. Ipsie seems less desirous of ferreting out a personally discovered Ipsie than of establishing an Ipsie or series of Ipsies to which she can hold in a bewildering world. Rodd, with his concern to find the real Ipsie, does not realize his mistake. Thus,

Without intending to show anything but his devotion, he [Rodd] came near to showing Ipsie that she would never find a perfect lover, and why. She became almost aware that her hunger for support was insatiable. . . . She sought praise of Rodd, despised him when he gave it and herself when he withheld it. Really she sought praise of herself and never found it. (PD, 149–50)

Her successful performance of the woman's role breeds in her contempt for the audience accepting her performance: an audience which is pleased by demonstrations of feminine traits. Unsuccessful performance simply underscores for her again her inability either to be what she wishes or to cover effectively her suppressed identity. She can never find praise of herself because her self must be hidden.

The self that Ipsie conceals is a self that seeks to embrace a wide range of experiences. It is not by accident that she thinks of her central control as masculine. Her Showman, her masculine element, directs her actions.

Were Ipsie to marry, there would be for a while the tension of two directing masculine egos: her Showman's and her husband's. Ipsie seems to believe that her husband would at last dominate and her Showman would leave her in peace. But the attraction of that peace wanes as it grows closer. To emphasize the horror for Ipsie of the role in which she had determined to imprison herself, Benson employs a brutal image as warning. Suspecting that her mission to rescue Jacob and reestablish herself as his beloved is after all a mistake, Ipsie is for the first time confronted not by the picturesque but by the grim reality of the world around her.

In the village they passed through, an idiot girl, suckling a baby, smiled through a harelip at the soldiers. The baby's eyes were black with flies. A dog that was scarcely alive writhed its cramped body into the sunlight. Men with sullen and debased faces looked from doorways, and the only pretty things the sun-light could find to play with were the intricately chased silver sheaths and hilts of the men's daggers. (PD, 164).

As this image suggests, motherhood will not automatically bring beatitude. Only decorations on instruments of aggression lend a kind of beauty to an otherwise sordid scene. This image is so telling because so unexpected. The reader is accustomed to descriptions of mountains, mountain people, and their costumes as vibrant with color and splendid with natural majesty. The world observed has been a delight to the eyes: the distinguishing characteristic of the setting of the novel is its nearly uninterrupted beauty. Thus, the stark description of the mindless mother and her doomed child contrasts jarringly with all that has preceded it and lingers in the mind as Ipsie rejects marriage and motherhood even should her partner be the pleasant Rodd. She chooses instead life with Pauline.

Pipers and a Dancer is not an apology for homosexuality; Benson merely claims for women what has earlier been the right of men. The ideal of perfect friendship had long been assumed to exist only between men. The true understanding of strong minds could be found among men—not between men and women, no matter how wise the woman, and certainly not between women. Benson's development of the bond between Pauline and Ipsie is handled quite skillfully: the sexual element is deemphasized and the emotional and social basis clarified. Thus, her handling of the bond between two women is quite different from D. H. Lawrence's as he develops the sensual nature of the bond between men in *Women in Love*, a novel published about the same time as *Pipers and a Dancer*.

Before she arrives in Hong Kong Ipsie is, for all her fragmented personality, quite conventional in her evaluation of the relative worth of men and women. For Ipsie, "Women were very seldom adventure. . . . The most one could say was that women were nothing at all in advance" (*PD*, 12). When she first meets the large and colorful Pauline and her withered companion Sophie Hinds, Ipsie notices that they seem to be a couple rather than two separate women. She notices that they "*flirted* with epigrams" (*PD*, 18; emphasis added). Later, while listening to Pauline explain Sophie's solicitude for Pauline's happiness, Ipsie is unimpressed, "though her Showman was careful to maintain in her face the sweet burning expression of one who discusses a love-affair" (*PD*, 50). Pauline, who had hoped that her brother would marry Sophie, explains that Jacob might have refused because

Sophie as a lover would have made most people feel inadequate. She has the same effect on me sometimes.
"Don't you think," said Ipsie. [*sic*] "That perhaps Mrs. Hinds thought marrying Jacob was the nearest she could get to marrying you, Pauline?"
Then Pauline knew definitely that she disliked Ipsie. (*PD*, 52–53)

Although Pauline herself could describe the lover-like relationship she has with Sophie, Ipsie has gone too far by recognizing the possibility of a desire for a parallel to heterosexual relationships. Pauline has established herself in a man's world and even enjoys the masculine prerogative of a collection of female admirers. The situation is not threatening to any of them because it is asexual:

Pauline, who did not impress men, considered it her right to possess all women. She disliked the institution of marriage. She was fond of telling women that she made a god of friendship and that, to such a god, sex played the part of devil. (*PD*, 53)

Pauline disavows the advantages of sex, and Sophie is living proof that one can, with proper control, remain remarkably innocent of the effects of physical contact. Mrs. Hind's husband had been "an increasingly inebriate travelling salesman. Her art and her devotion to two or three women friends had been her refuge. The refuge had shielded her not only from sorrow but from life. When her salesman died she was still spiritually a virgin" (*PD*, 89). Chaste friendship between women is offered as a protection against pain and can be a buffer against experience. But Ipsie's alliance with Pauline offers a broadening of experience. She will be able to exhibit all facets of her personality.

When Mary Hippolyta Wilson cries in Hong Kong "Oh my God, my God, where am I? Where is my dear self?" (*PD*, 64), she is addressing the stars. Later, she answers her own question: "I lost myself long ago. When I was born, I think." (*PD*, 116). This explanation should encourage the reader to examine not simply the person Ipsie, is, or could be, in isolation, but the problem that her necessary interaction with other people poses to her search for identity. Ipsie cannot establish her identity without considering those people who surround her. Ipsie initially might appear to be a hollow creature bowing to each new gust of wind, but closer examination reveals that she is not so much hollow as containing within a seed that cannot be allowed to flower because it would be unacceptable to the world in which she lives.

The poses that Ipsie rejects are all essentially feminine ones: she feels disgust as a wave of sweetness overcomes her while she adapts to the role of "sweet little thing" into which Pauline initially cast her. The role of a female Good Sport for Captain Norman is just as alien to her as "sweet little thing." She reflects upon the probable discomfort of courtesans while she is forced to lie in bed and be catered to as "Ipsie-wipsie," and the role of a wifely wee Mary is so alien that she cannot imagine Ipsie anywhere in a scene that contains wee Mary and her presumed domestic proficiency.

Furthermore, men do not find her attractive for long. Rodd had been attracted for two days, but once he began to know her, he found that Ipsie talked too much, over-explained, and tried too hard to be understood. Jacob had noticed this same characteristic and intended to break her of her habit of what he called nagging. Jacob recognizes her masculine inclination without consciously realizing it: although he usually talks about her as as a "cozy little body" and envisions her as soon to be a plump middle-aged matron, during the fever before his death he compares the pure Mary he intends to marry with the prostitute Maidie who deserted him. Maidie is the feminine figure and Mary is "small and bleak like a boy . . . a queer boy, the kind of boy you can't take into a bar" (*PD*, 130).

But perhaps more important than her absence of attraction for men is the fact that she does not seem to be at all attracted to them. Her contact with men and thoughts of men, with the exception of the ever-present awareness of the dead Conrad as Man, are usually unpleasant. She tries to ignore the real presence of Captain Norman when he kisses her. After the incident, when a momentary disappointment that Norman never actually tried to seduce her arises, Ipsie is struck by the complete artificiality of her concern. She thinks of Norman as a "stupid hairy stranger." Rodd almost did not exist for her, he inspired only a self-centered reaction: "She watched herself with outside eyes, she appraised herself with outside eyes, and now, being almost certain that Rodd valued her, she valued herself and, through herself, vaguely but delightfully valued him" (*PD*, 120). Rodd is, as a man, not attractive to her; he is valued as an appreciative audience. At best, "Men meant nothing to her, nothing more than Jacob Heming or Lord Salisbury or Anthony Trollope or the fishmonger, but Man she could see now with secret eyes, tall, pale-haired, thin and a little hesitating in the sentimental setting of a garden. . . . Part of his perfection was that he was a parody—in other words, a brother" (*PD*, 7).

Ellis Roberts recognizes that Ipsie's dead brother Conrad is important to an understanding of the novel, but he believes that there are not enough clues to decipher the importance. It is perfectly true that Ipsie's relationship with her brother is significant; with careful examination the reason becomes clear. Ipsie "did not consciously think a very great deal about Conrad now that he was dead . . . she had never confronted herself with the fact that actually he obsessed her. Only he was Man in the innocent, teeming world of her eyes" (*PD*, 9). Ipsie, whose poses are orchestrated by her inner Showman, seldom imitates her brother Conrad "because the natural Ipsie included so much of the natural Conrad that imitation was difficult" (*PD*, 58). Conrad does not represent an incestuous preoccupation, he represents her ideal self. She is obsessed with Conrad not because she loved him, but because she *knew* him. Ipsie longed not *for* her brother but to *be* her brother. Ipsie's fundamental dilemma is not that she is seeking a perfect man; she wishes to be a man.

Ipsie is reminded of her distaste for physical contact with men during the night she sleeps with Pauline on their way to meet the rescued Jacob:

"Dearest," said Pauline gently, stroking Ipsie's fingers under the blanket. "It has been a cloud, a blindness, that separated us. Love has triumphed." . . . Oblivion seemed to enclose Jacob and to detach his name from words. Ipsie could only think of the black hairs that grew in his ears. She wondered drearily what colour his pyjamas were. While Pauline stroked her fingers Ipsie hated all men—their hairiness, their coarseness of skin, their flannel pyjamas. . . . (*PD*, 168—70)

Ipsie's antipathy for men is clear, but she also disliked Pauline as long as she was "the prisoner of Pauline's favour" (*PD*, 166). Her antagonism continues as long as she is forced into accepting passive, essentially feminine roles from the capable and overpowering Pauline. It is not until

Pauline's formidable exterior weakens that Ipsie of her own volition initiates the union of Pauline and herself, and the first sign of her new attitude is the same physical contact which Pauline had made as they slept together.

Ipsie felt herself promoted as she stroked Pauline's hand. Here was a newly created Ipsie for the Showman—One who brings Comfort to the Weak and Sorrowful. Pauline was consenting to be weak and sorrowful. Now that Ipsie had seen Pauline surrendering there seemed to be nothing lacking about this wonderful woman. The essential inferiority of Pauline was at last hidden from Ipsie by Pauline's weakness. (*PD*, 176–77)

This is exactly what attracted the gardener to the suffragette in *I Pose* and what initiated Rodd's "love" for Ipsie: his recognition of her weakness. When Ipsie accepts Pauline, Ipsie is in the male-superior role. The small, twenty-four year old artist Ipsie "remembered with great pain the habitual arch and arbitrary expression of Pauline's eyes. Everything in the world seems worthless until that look should return to Pauline's eyes. 'Pauline . . . adorable, adorable Pauline'" (*PD*, 177). She can be for a while "One who brings Comfort," a Giver, to the tall, forty-three year old business woman Pauline. But she would not be restricted to that role, she could continue to be Pauline's dear little girlie—another version of wee Mary but without the restrictions that Jacob would have imposed upon her. This seems to be an androgynous union with both women capable and desirous of alternately fulfilling roles that are essentially masculine. That this is probably as close to an ideal relationship as either will ever come is emphasized by the cliché-ridden image that Pauline conjures for Ipsie.

Listen, we will go away by ourselves to Arizona and breathe the pure air into our lungs that are tired of China and get well and some day find our hearts healed again. Ah, the healing sunlight that is striped by the cactus shadows. . . . We will live on a ranch and milk cows and ride horses and wade in flowers. . . . Little sister. . . she smiles. . . she's *my* little girlie now. (*PD*, 177)

With Pauline, Ipsie will be tormented by neither a male identity repressed in a female body nor a female role played by a masculine sensibility. Her roles, her identity, will have complete freedom, and so the essential Ipsie, who is really nothing but the exploitation of all her possible identities, will at last be able to emerge.

Pipers and a Dancer is the first Benson novel to end with even a hint that the protagonist may find contentment through a union with another human being. Jay's marriage in *This Is the End* marks the surrender of what she believed to be her essential identity; hers is not a union of promise. Furthermore, the final chapter of that novel underscores the pathos of the empty, solitary Mr. Russell. *Pipers and a Dancer*, on the other hand, concludes with both Ipsie and Pauline anticipating a pleasant future and even Rodd, his vanity wounded, will be safe from the dangerous introspection that would have altered his own amiable self-image which he protects with his superficiality.

Benson's novels focus increasingly on the problem of women isolated in ill-fitting feminine roles. This is not a problem newly conceived, but its development has become more explicit. As early as *I Pose* the character of the suffragette, working for the improvement of the lot of women, claiming a right to the prerogatives of men, had been unable to join her life with the gardener's in a traditional effort to encourage mutual comfort. In *Pipers and a Dancer* Ipsie and Pauline seem well suited for each other, and their early ambivalence toward each other would not be at all unusual in a male-female relationship. Ipsie's rejection of Rodd and her conscious decision to accept Pauline may startle the reader into a closer examination of Ipsie's sense of absent identity. With this unconventional ending Benson encourages a questioning of convention. The determined preservation of individuality, even individuality characterized by an absence of defined identity, may ultimately make possible alliances against isolation.

Chapter Six
Exiles and Émigrés

Benson's last two novels are her finest work. They both continue to develop the subject of isolation in the world, and they both hold two worlds in suspension, but they are in fact quite different from each other in technique and theme. *Goodbye, Stranger* insists again that the reader enter a world of uncommon reality. The male central character is a changeling, a fairy in a man's body; but the reader is almost forced to consider the novel as a commentary on the sufficiency, or insufficiency, of stereotypes. *Tobit Transplanted*, on the other hand, is presented as a recording of mundane fact, but constructed as it is on the plot from the Apocrypha—a plot which contains an angel of God, a demon-haunted young woman, and miraculous cures—it prods the reader toward awe for the power of the human being to transcend usual physical and emotional rules.

Goodbye, Stranger

William Frierson has observed that the authors of the 1920s "cared little that [their] writing was true *to* life so long as it was true *of* life."[1] Stella Benson's *Goodbye, Stranger* illustrates this principle well. Concerned with problems of identity and isolation, the novel calls upon the world of fairies to demonstrate the truth of the human world. As the reviewer in the London *Times* recognized, Benson's subject is "the clash of two worlds. Like another poet turned novelist, Mr. De la Mare, she always inhabits two worlds at once, and like him she uses some oddity brought from the other world as a touchstone to prove the nature of this. It is a method that will serve for satire or for tragedy, and these writers use it for both. In this fashion the novel becomes otherworldly without ceasing to deal with matters of fact; it moves nearer to poetry."[2] *Goodbye, Stranger*, like good poetry, turns the reader back upon himself and reveals an increased complexity with each reading.

The novel covers a thirty-six hour period while three female English performers are in a Chinese town. The town boasts, in addition to a few Frenchmen, an English missionary family named Lorne, Clifford Cotton and his American wife Daley and his mother, and three single men:

Lion, Mr. Diamond, and a doctor. Lena, one of the performers, has an attack of pleurisy during the evening performance and is taken to the house of Daley and Clifford Cotton. Daley is shallow but pretty, pleasant, and kind. Her husband Clifford believes that he is a changeling, a fairy who has inhabited a man's body for seven years. His goal in life is to be at home in the world, and he believes Lena has a wisdom that she can share with him and that will allow him to attain his goal. Clifford makes no secret of his fascination with Lena, who is seldom sought after by men and is usually unpopular with women. Attracted to Daley, Lena accepts Clifford's advances while Daley tries to overlook his obsession with the haggard, sexless woman. Even when Daley sees Clifford emerging late at night from Lena's room, rather than question him she spends the night and part of the next day trying to avoid the truth of the sexual encounter between her husband and her invalid house guest.

The next morning Lena all but explicitly admits the affair in an effort to focus Daley's attention on herself. Later repenting the indiscretion, she sends a note to Daley asking her to come to her room. Unfortunately, when Daley arrives Clifford is embracing Lena, and he unabashedly announces that he loves her but would like Daley to remain with them. Daley runs out of the house, and Clifford the changeling is sent away by Lena.

Daley returns home by dinner time, but Clifford remains absent. Soon most of the local community is trying to protect Daley from their suspicion that Clifford has either gone mad or been murdered. His clothes have been found in a bamboo grove, and he has been seen running naked in the woods. What actually happened was that the changeling discarded his clothing and was reclaimed by his fairy people. The person who finally returns late at night to Daley is her seven-years-absent husband. Lena discovers the changeling's departure when old Mrs. Cotton enters Lena's room to bemoan the return of the *"so* manly—*so* practical—*so* good-hearted . . . fool"[3] who is her son, and the departure of the fairy who had occupied her son's body.

Benson believed that her thesis was quite clear. It was, in her later opinion, too clear: "In writing *Goodbye, Stranger*, I forgot my dislike of taking sides—and the book is unfortunately full of personal bias and personal appeals, with a refrain of This is Right, and This is Wrong which I now think most unnecessary."[4] But with this remark she was underestimating her accomplishment. The simplistic thesis Benson seems to have believed she was developing, a thesis which asserts that there is a Right and a Wrong, is contrary to the thesis that in fact emerges. As one reviewer noted, "Goodness is a quality for which, in her last book, she seems to be making a haphazard search: but whenever she comes upon its likeness she points rudely and makes faces at it."[5] But Benson does not carelessly make faces and flit on. Studying what life offers, she always discovers some qualifying element which will not allow her to believe that she has at last discovered an absolute good. Thus, what is true of life is true of the novel: general observations are easy to make, but precise, accurate, comprehensive judgments are quite difficult.

Goodbye, Stranger is a more mature presentation of Benson's earlier preoccupations. There is a world-weary response to the dilemma of identity which strips away any shred of optimism in the reader's response, yet offers a more positive, realistic assessment of the world. Any reader of Benson's earlier novels will recognize in the character of Lena the later life of earlier heroines. Lena is alone, and apparently alone by choice, and she reaffirms that choice after her experience with the changeling Clifford. True, just before learning that the changeling has been returned to his fairy people, Lena looks to the mountains and wills Clifford to return to her. However, she makes absolutely no physical move to encourage him to come to her. Furthermore, she does not pretend to herself that she is being swept by a strong emotion. She is in command of herself and would like Clifford on her terms, but she will not risk any shadow over her independence by pursuing him or even overtly indicating her interest in him. Her independence may seem comfortless, and indeed Lena is cold and dry herself, but, again, it is worth stressing that the life she leads is a life she chooses.

Benson's heroines, unlike Virginia Woolf's upper-class or upper-middle-class women, are not totally divorced from the need for money. Nor are they, though, driven to act because of a need for money. Even Lena, who is closer to destitution than any of Benson's earlier heroines, seems indifferent to her financial situation. Benson's women all seem to come from that genteel class that assumes their daughters will dutifully marry but that finds many of their young women husbandless in the work force. These women are not faced with the choice of husbands or sweatshops, although the decision to work is probably assumed to be an admission of failure to secure a proposal. One always has the feeling that if Benson's women did not choose to work there would be families, heretofore ignored, ready to reembrace the prodigal daughter. But it is the reader's vague sense of the safety net beneath these solitary women that places emphasis on the fact of their choice. In this novel above all else Benson makes the point of the possibility of female independence.

This is not, however, a one point book. While insisting upon the possibility of female independence, Benson demonstrates the inadequacy, indeed the destructiveness, of the feminine stereotype both for the women who strive to embody it and the men who must then live with women intent upon passivity, submission, and rejection of their physical or intellectual natures. Meanwhile, as she explores the recesses of isolation in the world, Benson weaves in a criticism of commercialism and the cult of mediocrity spreading out from the United States.

It is the disinclination or inability to accept the combined physical, emotional, and intellectual components of a relationship or even of one's own personality that contributes most significantly to the pervasive sense of isolation in the novel. For instance, the missionary couple, the Lornes, are finally isolated from each other because Mr. Lorne cannot share the emotional life of his wife and Mrs. Lorne cannot find beauty in their sexual life.

Embodying the matronly ideal, self-effacing Mrs. Lorne loves her children and is always ready to serve when needed. Her husband seems to be a genuinely holy man; however, he leaves his wife to face the death of their infant son alone: the baby's dying gasps are too painful for him to hear. Not only does he abandon his wife at her most soul-wrenching hour, he is unable to comfort her. In fact, he is unaware of the extent of her misery. Crying inwardly for her dead son but ashamed of her feeling, Mrs. Lorne is locked in her misery by the *belief* that she ought to accept God's will and the *reality* that her bereavement is unassuaged. She is unable to communicate her pain to her husband. Furthermore, when her husband tries to communicate his fears and longings to her, she is unable to offer him comfort because what he asks involves a rejection of one component of the ideal female stereotype.

Mrs. Lorne, nearly broken by the death of an infant, is unable to accept lovingly the physical act that produces her children, the objects of her love. Even with her own husband she is embarrassed when the conversation turns to sex. Believing "it was coarse to talk about birth or begetting," this mother of several children, who is silently but constantly mourning the death of her son, withdraws her hand from the arm of her husband when he cries, as they walk through a wood at night, "It is not true, that bodies are only seducers of the virgin soul. It is not true that souls are always ravished virgins and bodies always legalised seducers. Marriage between the body and soul is honourable, in the sight of God. And we have achieved it, Constance, haven't we—haven't we?" (*GS*, 269). In spite of years of marriage and holy intentions, this pious couple has not achieved a marriage of the body and soul. They are victims of the convention that dictates that women endure sex to please husbands and beget children. They will walk through life as they left that moonlit wood, "two separate oblong shadows" (*GS*, 269).

On the other hand, Daley and Clifford Cotton enjoy the union of their bodies, but for seven years there has been no mutual emotional and intellectual commitment in their marriage. It is because of the absence of anything but physical pleasure in Clifford's response to her, that Daley is so bewildered when she sees her husband attracted to the unfeminine Lena. "We often loved each other. I couldn't have lived without. . . . Love only means one thing to him, really; it never before now meant anything so silly as wisdom . . . he doesn't allow anything in love but nature" (*GS*, 247, 246).

Unlike Mrs. Lorne, Daley can embrace without embarrassment the physical side of love. Indeed, since that is all she has of her husband, she can let that be sufficient to maintain her emotional commitment. Tenderness from her husband she imagines when she is alone, and the fantasy, the quiet pretense that he feels all that she wishes he would say to her, sustains her.

The critic for the *Saturday Review* thought Daley an "amiable but not very consistent character." He went on to explain, "It is one of Miss Benson's shortcomings that she cannot bring herself to let the stupid stew quietly in their stupidity; ever and again a bubble of wit disturbs their viscous surface."[6] But the reviewer missed the point. Although Daley is not an introvert inclined to self-doubt or intellectual pondering, she is not stupid. She has a mind but does not bother to use it.

Daley, "full of life, healthy, ignorant and humble," is vibrantly alive physically yet unaware of her own capacity for intellectual activity. "Her brains had scarcely furnished her mind at all—and yet she had a vividly lighted mind. A springtime breeze had blown innocent visions through the bright rooms of her mind. . . . Nothing inside the house of her mind had ever seemed to her very seriously wrong—not because she had searched and found everything perfect, but because she had never searched at all" (*GS*, 253). Daley is an innocent, kind-hearted young woman who, when confused by the dazzle of a husband or a world she does not understand, hopes for the best and works for the best, and finds innocent comfort from her pets and the admiring men around her.

Daley is encouraged in her childishness by the men in her life who find her sweet, pretty, and safe. Their admiration for her runs no serious risk of bringing them unwelcome responsibility. She is actually quite important to them because she permits them to act out their protective fantasies, thereby bolstering their self-images. Mr. Diamond can imagine himself strong and paternal toward her. Lion can be lovelorn while dreaming about life in Canada with and without Daley, and her husband may be lord of his household as his wife overlooks his callousness and his mother approves of the unhappiness he causes his wife.

Because her husband doesn't value her the way magazine advertisements suggest she should be valued, and because he seems oblivious to the mild flirtations other men indulge themselves with her, Daley has no anchored sense of identity. She needs the admiration of men just as much as the men need her for their pretense of love. With no sense of independent identity or inner resources to establish her own worth apart from the value bestowed by men, Daley constantly searches for her importance in the eyes of others. Therefore, when aware that she is being ignored, Daley warbles out her desire for attention. A less charming person would be criticized for her inability to be interested in others. In another environment Daley's childlike nature would become first cloying, then tiresome, but as the only attractive female among several men she receives the pampering that allows her to be lovable.

Although pampered by the men in her community, Daley feels fundamentally lost. Her worldly importance is established by her relation to men, and she is in a sense isolated from all the men around her. She is isolated from her husband by his lack of interest in her and from the other men by her determination to maintain her identity as Mrs. Cotton. With no inner anchor she relies heavily on outer aspect. It is significant that Daley does not think of herself as a person. Her essential self, in her own mind, is her reflection in a mirror. As Patricia Spacks has pointed out in her study *The Female Imagination*, women's identification of themselves with their image in a mirror is a recurring motif in women's fiction. What the world sees of them is important. And the world, of course, is men. For Daley women have no significance beyond their potential threat to her reign over the men around her. Old Mrs. Cotton is a constant criticizer who relishes Daley's dismay at her changeling, but Mrs. Cotton is unimportant: Clifford is no more considerate of her feelings than he is of Daley's.

By failing to develop an appreciation for her own mind and her own ability to establish standards for judgment, Daley becomes an eternal child. Although her childlike engagement in life follows a superficial romantic tradition of wonder at nature, truly Romantic awareness of the awfulness of nature is noticeably absent. Attractive, unfailingly compassionate, harmlessly self-centered though lamentably lacking in self-awareness, Daley is, as Lena notices, "a typical man's woman" (*GS*,

119). Physically and emotionally alive, Daley ignores her intellectual potential.

Lena, on the other hand, is all too aware of the immensity and terror the world holds and all too conscious of her own mind. Lena is neither a man's woman like Daley nor a woman's woman like Sophie Hinds in *Piper and a Dancer*; she is simply her own self. Well, not quite. Lena's emotional life is so stifled that even her physical life is affected. Pain is ever present; pleasure is never admitted without reservation.

Although Lena lacks "vitality enough to understand him, or even love him" (*GS*, 25), Clifford turns to her for wisdom because she is a person who is not pleased with her sickly exterior, who obviously dwells deep within herself, and who also obviously does not expect the good of the world to fall in her lap, as Daley does. But Lena's misery seems to be more than the result of precariously maintained health. Though she does indulge in self-pity, she is less like Edward in *The Poor Man* than like Ipsie in *Pipers and a Dancer*. Lena, like Ipsie, seems to be plagued by a masculine sensibility in a female (though not feminine) body.

Lena "felt more at ease with women than with men and rather liked saying flattering—even sometimes almost loverlike—things to women" (*GS*, 96). Lena's reaction to Daley is certainly loverlike. When she first meets Daley, Lena's only thought is "'I wish I needn't be hiding my life from her. I wish I were eighteen again and a virgin. . . .' She wished that Daley would die this minute and so smile at Lena, as it were for ever" (*GS*, 14−15). That is not the conventional woman-to-woman reaction, and the absence of an exclusive femininity in Lena is not lost upon the young bachelor Lion or upon Daley. Lion felt physically repelled by Lena, and Daley, noticing Lena smile at her with "a boy's smile," thought, "I wouldn't like to undress in front of her, somehow. She's not a woman at all. No harm in that. Clifford can't go on forever looking at an imitation boy" (*GS*, 57). But it is the fact that Lena *is* an imitation boy that draws the changeling Clifford to her. He equates wisdom with knowing how to be at home in the world, and he seems to recognize that Lena is *not* comfortable with her place in the world although she has apparently managed to adjust herself to her unacceptable identity.

Attracted to women and resembling a boy, with a frail body but a strong mind, Lena suffers not from her sexual indulgences but from her sexual repressions. Although "manly humour, bar-humour, consisting largely of jokes dealing with water-closets, double beds and the accidental disclosing of undressed ladies, seemed, though disconcerting, very vital and exciting" to Lena, she had maintained an affair with a "thin, Fulham Poet . . . whose only dissipation was a refined use of a mild drug, and whose obscenities were so excessively psychological" (*GS*, 26). The manly humor she enjoys would be scarce with her dissipated poet. However, life with this effete man might be as close as she has come to being the lover of a woman: the affair may have been her compromise between her attraction to women and convention's demand that she prefer men. By denying her sexual inclinations Lena protected herself from life with negatives.

Incapable of either loving Clifford or attracting Daley, Lena has committed what Mr. Lorne the missionary believes to be the fatal error: "not to be alive, not to let life in, is to accept corruption—it is worse than wickedness. Yes, that is the One Sin" (*GS*, 57). Remembering the night she spent with Clifford, Lena thinks of him as a flame, yet he did not burn her soul. She recognized that he was a glory come into her life, yet she felt no glow or tumult. Lena knows herself too well and thus finds herself unable to respond with abandon to the physical pleasure Clifford brings her.

Clifford the changeling has a physical and literally honest response to life. His actions lack the softening influence of emotion and the qualification of intellectual direction. He is aware of an absence in himself; he has spent seven years seeking wisdom, but he seems incapable of doing anything more than simply being. His physical presence and sense of being alien to his environment constitute his sense of self. Emotional involvement seems to have been left out of his makeup. He is equally bereft of wisdom, which he hopes to find, much like one might find a lost wallet. He seems to regard wisdom as a thing or a trick, not a condition arrived at through mental effort.

The various attractions among these characters and the obstacles to their unions develop another motif of this novel: not only are individuals isolated from each other, they are fundamentally lost to themselves. A perfect balance of heart, mind, and body should be natural but seems impossible to achieve.

Daley is dominated by her heart. She can respond with full emotion to the world around her; she can accept and rejoice in the physical nature of life, but she is an unsatisfying companion because intellect is foreign to her. Daley comes close to being the ideal female according to nineteenth- and early twentieth-century convention, but as with most stereotypes, she would be found wanting in an important area of her personality. In this case her complete absence of intellection would gradually leave her with little to hold a husband's affections. Mrs.

Bennett in Jane Austen's *Pride and Prejudice* became a trial to her husband as her youthful beauty faded and her intellectual weakness became more apparent. This is the fate that awaits Daley. Daley is a representative of empty-headed Americanism and also quiescent womanhood, both criticized by Benson. But she is also sympathetic, caring, and naturally good. The character embodying the traits Benson criticizes most is developed very sympathetically. But it takes little imagination to realize that an older Daley will be simply another silly, sentimental woman.

In contrast to Daley, Lena is a woman of acute self-awareness, a woman who has withdrawn to her own mind. Her emotional reserve and unfeminine exterior attract Clifford Cotton, a man surfeited with love and beauty from his wife. Irritated, puzzled, and excited by Clifford, Lena can appreciate his physical power without being swept up in the emotion that power usually engenders. The Clifford who seeks her out she can understand and send away; the Clifford she doesn't understand she hopes will return. But the very source of Lena's attraction, her wisdom which puts her outside the conventional feminine image, drives away the changeling, the being who thought he was prepared to take chances in his search for wisdom. Confronting a critical intelligence he is literally stripped bare. The changeling Clifford Cotton was seen running naked in the woods just before he returned to his original world. His physical nakedness images the interior nakedness illuminated by his contact with Lena. The unsettling presence of an independent woman drives off the changeling in Clifford and restores to Daley her appreciative, manly husband. He has found it much safer and more comforting to accept than to question.

Clifford the changeling is above all conscious of his physical presence. Lamenting his absence of wisdom he labors to acquire the physical mannerisms that characterize those people who have a clear sense of identity. His physical force gives pleasure to Daley but cannot by itself bring her happiness. She is lonely and confused as long as her husband avoids emotional engagement. Lena recognizes Clifford's physical nature but is unswayed by it; it is the mystery of the changeling, not the strength of the man, that fascinates her.

When Clifford the man returns to his wife after seven years, he returns to a woman who has lived with unhappiness and has been bombarded with cynicism, but who has maintained a love for and interest in life and the pure joy of experience. The reader is relieved and happy that Daley has found again the husband who completely and conventionally loves her. Yet, in spite of old Mrs. Cotton's maliciousness and Lena's dessicated life, there is an ambivalence in the reader's mind, a reluctant admission that though "perhaps the world's a little better for the loss of a stony-hearted fairy," Mrs. Cotton is right when she mourns the fact that "there are so many men, and—so—few—fairies" (*GS*, 297). A little less summer sunlight in the mind and a little more dark night of the soul might be a welcome influence.

While developing the broad comment on fragmented identity and individual isolation, *Goodbye, Stranger* follows the pattern of the quest myth to comment on the threat that women who are not passive and demure pose to men. This story makes perfect sense as an allegory criticizing society's roles for men and women. Daley seems the perfect wife and woman, but the shallows of her mind tire her husband. Clifford Cotton, secure in the approval of his mother (who seems to encourage his less-than-loving treatment of his wife) and the loyalty of his wife, is free to test the role of seeker. As a man he may openly demand more from life than what he has. Tired of seeing his reflection in the adoring gaze of his wife, he may search for a more critical view, a more complex image. During this time he is not the contented man he was but a man callous to the feelings of his wife. However, his chafing at his sane and sensible marriage and his adoring wife evaporates once he has glimpsed life with a woman who does *not* reflect his desires. Finally meeting a woman who does not consider him all-important—a sexually experienced, economically independent, emotionally ambivalent, and physically weak woman who, attracted to his wife, does not abandon herself to him—he withdraws from the search for wisdom. The wisdom he would find would diminish his stature in his own eyes. He has been all-important to his wife and mother: he is not even able to give Lena self-forgetting pleasure. The wisdom that comes with the realization that one is not all-perfect requires more strength than many men have. Clifford becomes again the happily married man, content to see himself reflected in Daley's uncritical eyes.

In addition to the problems of sex stereotypes, the phenomenon of modern commercial America disturbed Benson greatly. Her concern is reflected in both her professional writing and her personal correspondence. She made no secret of her distaste for the "modern expression of democracy—especially intellectual democracy";[7] earlier criticism is found in *The Poor Man* and several of her short stories. But one of the great strengths of *Goodbye, Stranger* is the fact that she does not encrust any single character with so much criticism that he or she loses all sympathy. Benson is evenhanded in her criticism if restrained in her admiration. This trait is nowhere more clearly seen than in her handling of the character of Daley Cotton.

Daley is an American who reads American magazines and tries to make an American home of a household in China consisting of her changeling husband who has no consideration for her feelings and her detestable English mother-in-law. Her wistful longing for the life depicted in magazine advertisements is her expression of unhappiness as she remains loyal to a man who for seven years has seemed indifferent to her happiness. In spite of her years of unhappiness, Daley remains superficial and innocent. This representative of the oft-criticized American culture embodies the positive that may also be found in that culture. When she defends America while admitting that she does not have the greatness of the best Americans, her defense of America is more lethal for America than the cruel and self-centered Mrs. Cotton's worst diatribes against American mediocrity.

Think of all the inspiring messages flying about in the air of America—all the deep helpful thoughts about theosophy and the message of the Great War to future generations and psycho-analysis and Rabindranath Tagore and how one can bring the spirit of Jesus into business. I think it's just fine that deep constructive thinking should be so popular—the favourite indoor sport of a great country like America . . . your European way of just sitting back and registering cynicism is such an *easy* way: Americans are strenuous people and they despise easy ways. Not *me* of course. . . . I've lost the knack of high helpful thinking. I think about insects and dogs and what it would feel like to be a queen . . . or a dipsomaniac . . . or a sea-anemone when a big wave's coming. (GS, 194)

Daley, the product of American culture, is sensitive to life around her. Her absence of high helpful thinking does not prevent her from bringing a spirit of life and compassion to her surroundings, a spirit regrettably absent in many high thinkers who are uninspired to equally positive actions. Unfortunately, simply thinking great thoughts without incorporating the conclusions in practical actions will not do the world much good. Furthermore, as Daley correctly observes, "your European way of just sitting back and registering cynicism is such an *easy* way." Cynicism might be a refuge for the lucky, but the European habit of believing the worst is no more helpful than the American habit of thinking the best: action is necessary.

The thirty-six hour period covered in the novel is significant for Daley and Clifford Cotton; it is of no great moment for Lena. Daley's husband is returned to her and the couple face an amiable future bound by affection and physical desire. If mental activity is lacking, probably neither will notice. Daley has never been aware of a need for thought or introspection, and her husband has realized he is not prepared to follow the lonely, tortuous road to wisdom. If mental activity is absent from their relationship, neither will regret its absence.

For Lena this time has not marked a crisis in her life. This is the sort of interlude that is almost inevitable given her circumstances and experiences. She is a woman no longer young who is earning a rather precarious living but who feels no urgent need to change her circumstances. Lena is not searching for her identity, she is not questioning herself, she is not facing a crisis either emotional or financial. Her experience with the Cottons is neither a beginning nor an ending, it will not affect her for the rest of her life.

Although her sympathies are with Lena, Benson is not uncritical, and she emphasizes that there is much in life that Lena misses. To develop that point Benson creates a claustrophobic setting for Lena. All the action in Lena's life seems to take place in the evening and at night, and an imprisoning rain seems to surround her. Daley, on the other hand, moves outside and searches the world around her for beauty and comfort. The effects of rain surround her when she is outside; the world for Daley seems new and sunny even when human comfort is absent.

The pervasive isolation of individuals is apparent when the identity of the stranger of the title is sought. The most obvious candidate is the changeling Clifford, the fairy stranger in the real world who, after his contact with Lena, returns to his fairy world. The title could be a farewell to the changeling. A second possibility is that the title could refer to Lena, who is from the beginning of the novel a stranger. When the man Clifford Cotton returns to his wife he is someone to whom the frail boyish body of Lena will be forever a stranger. Lena, a stranger to life who has erected so many defenses that the extremes of joy and sorrow are lost to her, will leave the house and lives of the Cottons. Her physical intimacy with the body of the fairy Clifford Cotton will be unremembered by the man, and her attraction to Daley will never even have been recognized by anyone other than herself. Thus, the novel's title may be a sardonic farewell to a woman who has been and will be everywhere a stranger. There is a third possibility. With the return of the human Clifford who disappeared seven years earlier, Daley is no longer a stranger among cynics. Her husband is not seeking wisdom, and he is delighted with his pretty, childlike wife. He may bridge the gap between Daley's innocence and her neighbors' disillusion. The title may allude to the renewed bond between husband and wife which banishes the confused and estranged Daley and replaces her with a contented and loved woman. These three possibilities are not mutually exclusive; indeed, they are held simultaneously.

Still Benson demonstrates that women *can* be independent; they can be sufficient unto themselves. She makes no attempt to suggest that the life of the single woman is gay or that it is tragic; it is lonely and even dangerous, but it is an alternative that women are capable of electing and preferring.

Goodbye, Stranger is a truly remarkable book which draws upon the supernatural to insist upon the realities of our own world. The element of fantasy enables Benson to emphasize the situation of the women while minimizing a reader's desire to defend the man involved. The fact that Daley's husband is temporarily non-human frees the reader from any inclination to discover a misunderstood or much suffering husband. And of course the fact that he is non-human establishes a disequilibrium in the reader. The constant necessity of trying to place this odd creature finally underscores the external ordinariness of the situation: a man insensitive to the emotions of his pleasant, boring wife rediscovers her value after his experience with a woman of more independent mind. Because Benson supplies an excuse for the man, the reader can more readily sympathize with the woman. The exotic setting and the intrusion of fairies and changelings in the lives of mortals develop a criticism of blind adherence to approved roles and acknowledge the difficulty of independence.

Tobit Transplanted

Tobit Transplanted (published in America as *The Far Away Bride*) was critically and financially Stella Benson's most successful novel. In 1932 it won both the A. C. Benson silver medal for "services to literature" and the Vie Heureuse Prize—a French honor which thrilled her more than the English recognition. For *Tobit Transplanted* Benson transformed the story of Tobit in the Apocrypha, with its magic, devil, and angel, and produced a rationally explicable tale in which there is no necessarily supernatural power; there is only the awesome and mysterious power of each individual mind upon itself, upon the body that houses it, and upon the lives that swirl around it.

Seryozha Malinin, a Russian youth of eighteen living in Manchuria with his blind father and well-meaning but undignified mother, is sent by his father to Seoul, Korea, to collect a two-hundred-yen debt. A young Chinese man who studied law in England is providentially found to accompany Seryozha to Seoul. The Chinese guide, Wilfred Chew (C'hu Wei-fu), is to receive a fixed sum plus expenses and a commission on all money he retrieves over the two hundred yen of the original ten-year-old loan.

Wilfred Chew, formerly of Middle Temple, London, has no apparent means of support; and as he and his charge walk toward Seoul, he formulates a plan to marry Seryozha to the daughter of a rich Russian who lives in a village just twelve hours' walk out of the way. This beautiful young girl has been engaged to seven different young men and has broken each of the engagements. Tanya Ostapenko's effect on each of the young men has been disastrous. They were all respectable when they met her; now an alcoholic, a pimp in Shanghai, a member of the Chinese army, and even a soon-to-be suicide are among her rejected suitors. To the enormous disappointment of her prosperous father and the concern of her solitary mother, Tanya feels no desire for human companionship. "To be approached was entirely unbearable; a desiring or acute glance was in itself an assault; see she must, but to be seen was somehow insult. She loathed touch and always avoided it; the lightest accidental touch rasped her like a cat's tongue."[8] Wilfred Chew has heard of the girl's reputation as a cold woman delivering misfortune to her suitors, so when on their way to Seoul Seryozha catches a salmon, Chew has him save the heart, liver, and gall. The smoke from the heart and liver, he informs Seryozha, will cure the coldness in a woman, and putrified fish gall will cure most cases of blindness. The Wesleyan-indoctrinated Mr. Chew does not attribute this remedy to superstition but proven Chinese medical practice.

When the two travellers reach Mi-san where the Ostapenkos live, they are invited in to dinner and to spend the night. Seryozha, discovered to be the son of a cousin of Mr. Ostapenko, is welcomed as a member of the family. Champagne, to which Mr. Chew is unaccustomed but which he inadvertently drinks, flows freely. While Tanya is in the kitchen assisting in the preparations for dinner, Seryozha throws pieces of the fish liver and heart on the kitchen fire. By midnight Wilfred Chew has, unbidden, drawn up a marriage contract which includes a provision for an agent's fee for him and a large dowry for Seryozha. Tanya, her father, and Seryozha sign the contract while Chew lies unconscious at the table. Convincing both himself and Seryozha that the contract is legal, Pavel Ostapenko assures the young man that he is now married and sends him to Tanya's bedroom. Seryozha takes with him what remains of the liver and heart of the fish to put on the fire in her room.

During the night Pavel Ostapenko, overcome by the fear that the boy will be discovered dead in the morning, digs a grave which he joyfully orders his Korean gardener to fill when the couple emerges, alive and apparently happy, the next day. While the bride and groom wait with her family, Wilfred Chew travels to Seoul and collects the two hundred yen plus interest, which was the original aim of their journey.

When the young couple and Wilfred Chew finally return to Kanto and Seryozha's parents, they bring with them considerable wealth. Seryozha, who immediately rubs the fish gall on his father's eyes, is credited with restoring his father's sight. Mr. Chew, when offered a reward above the agreed-upon commission for his several additional accomplishments, refuses it saying he was acting as an angel of God. He takes only his commission and leaves. Seryozha, a young man entering a new maturity with a new wife, has returned to a home with a nagging father and an impetuous mother, both of whom love him immensely and see him as forever a child.

Tobit Transplanted is Stella Benson's greatest literary achievement. Broader in subject and less aggressively defensive than her earlier works, it is, she thought, a "kind" book. By removing the supernatural explanation for the miracles in the original story, she increases the importance of the individual and his effect upon himself and others. All the miracles are the result of strong convictions within individuals operating upon those individuals and the people around them. The setting and nationalities of the characters emphasize the theme of isolation; the complexity of the characters moderates that isolation.

The characters in this novel grow and change. Always before the characters in Benson's novels seem to reaffirm what they are at the beginning; the significant development has been the resistance to change, regardless of the inducement. Benson allows her characters in this novel scope to expand their borders and include others as citizens of their kingdoms of the self. Tanya and Seryozha begin the novel isolated and quite content in their isolation. Preferring their comfortable self-centeredness they nonetheless do change as they commit themselves to each other. However, the marriage will not create two beings with identical goals and strengths. Benson emphasizes this point by exploring the marriages of the young couple's parents. Recognizing essential individuality, Benson demonstrates the possibility of a common ground upon which two people may meet and strengthen each other. This is not, however, a rosy-hued sentimental novel. The comfort found in loyalty and self-interested affection springs always from pity. Yet Benson never allows the pathetic to lodge itself in the action; she utilizes her always remarkable talent for telling observations and reveals mastery of full-bodied comedy glimpsed but never developed in earlier works which are buoyed along with irony and understatement.

The story from the Apocrypha upon which this novel is based explicitly identifies magic—or the direct intervention of God—as the source of the marvelous happenings which conspire to answer the prayers of a blind old man and a husbandless though much-engaged young girl. Benson adheres faithfully to the details of the story, which she reproduces as an appendix to her novel. However, without changing any detail of the plot except the nationality and location of the characters, she offers a modern account of interesting coincidences surrounding significant events that may all be explained in terms of psychological cause and effect.

Old Sergei Malinin becomes blind soon after his failed shopkeeping enterprise is raided by Chinese soldiers angered by his defense of dead Russian soldiers and immediately after he defies the Chinese police and buries the body of a drunken Russian saddle-maker. Sergei claims sparrow dung fell in his eyes during the night and blinded him; the Japanese doctor who examines him claims the blindness is caused by hysteria. Being blind does enable him to shift responsibility for the family fortunes to his wife and son. His sight is completely restored after his son rubs the putrified gall of a long-dead fish in his eyes. It is, however, worth noting that by the time of his cure Old Sergei knows his son has married the only child of a prosperous man; Sergei can be reasonably certain that his financial worries are over. Furthermore, Sergei has had two flashes of sight before he is smeared in the awful mess his son has brought to cure him. Sergei's favorite activity had long been to honor the dead. Indeed, that practice was the immediate cause of his declining fortunes and his loss of sight. Accompanying Anna to the wake of a young man who committed suicide, Sergei actually sees the corpse, although he is not conscious that he is seeing at the time. Finally, before Seryozha reaches his father to apply the fish gall, under the excitement of the news that his son is returning, Sergei is already regaining his sight. This seems convincing evidence that the Japanese doctor was right: the blindness was caused by a psychological rather than a physical problem. Sergei Malinin's desire to escape responsibility was strong enough to deprive him of his eyesight.

Seryozha's angel of God is, like the cure of Sergei's blindness, rationally explicable. At the age of thirteen C'hu Wei-fu was sent to a mission school to learn English, become a Christian, and thus secure life's advantages. Under the tutelage of the Reverend Oswald Fawcett, Wilfred Chew's (C'hu Wei-fu) "naturally affectionate heart" grew and inspired in him a desire "to *be* good—not only to *seem* good" (*TT*, 97). His goal in life is to be a good Christian and a good businessman. Though he does not always see a contradiction in these goals, his Wesleyan background, in the form of the memory of the Reverend Oswald Fawcett, rises to haunt him at moments when a questionable profit might be realized. So Wilfred Chew, overcome by his desire to be good, convinces himself that he is in fact God's messenger and cannot accept an earthly reward for doing God's will. Content with his commission, Wilfred rejects Sergei's offer of a bonus for all that he has accomplished.

Wilfred Chew embraces the spirit of Christianity with a fervor found most often in converts. His mind produces not a physical blindness but a commercial myopia. Facing an uncertain future, he places himself and his fate in God's hands and rejects material security. This action produces a great feeling of self-satisfaction as it allows him to convince himself that he is, after all, "a great sinner used as a divine mouthpiece—a Chinese Saint Paul" (*TT*, 337).

Similarly, Tanya's apparent frigidity seems much less likely to have been caused by her possession by a demon than by her life with her mother and the fact that her suitors were physically unattractive to her. Tanya's mother was certainly not a woman who would be able to encourage her daughter to yield herself to male entreaties. Mrs. Ostapenko "had no illusions about the incompleteness of her own nature, though she would have resented bitterly any suggestion that an outsider could see her lack of life" (*TT*, 220). Although she has tried to hide her distaste for physical contact, her husband admits to Seryozha that he has been wounded throughout their marriage by her inadequate responses to his sexual advances. A woman whose "natural instinct" under the best of circumstances would be "to lie awake with tears of horror throughout her daughter's wedding night" (*TT*, 221) would be quite likely to have a daughter who screams when a young man tries to kiss her or bites when he tries to caress her hand. Furthermore, although Tanya's reactions to the physical attentions of her former suitors were certainly extreme, the reader *does* get the distinct impression that, in love though these suitors may have been, attractive they were not. While fixing dinner after Seryozha's arrival Tanya thinks of him, remembering that "the skin at the back of his neck was not pitted or pimpled like Sasha's or Petya's. This meant a great deal." (*TT*, 160). She has apparently not found any of the other young men physically attractive. Naturally she might not have been eager for physical contact with them.

That Tanya could accept and respond to Seryozha is quite explicable without recourse to exorcism. Just before Seryozha arrives, the Ostapenkos learn that one of Tanya's rejected suitors has killed himself. She is then subjected to the verbal and physical abuse of her father who is frustrated and frightened by his daughter who seems so unnatural in her repelling of young men and so indifferent to their eventual fate. In addition, because of a confusion with Wilfred Chew, her father pours Tanya champagne early in the evening. Under the influence of champagne her response to Seryozha seems cozily asexual as they gaze across the table in a "mindless drowsy warmth of shared life . . . as deeply sunk in themselves and in each other as puppies must feel in one litter in the straw while the bustle of the stable goes on above them" (*TT*, 205). The eventual outcome is not really surprising. A young girl with a frigid mother and unattractive former suitors has been subjected to a torrent of parental reproach on the subject of her cold nature and husbandless future. Under the combined influence of heady wine, an attractive stranger, a providential proposal, and an approving, enthusiastic father, she agrees to marry and apparently discovers that the sexual experience is not as horrible as she feared it would be. As Tanya later admits to his mother, Seryozha is physically beautiful. The fish heart and liver burned to drive away the devil which Seryozha believed was making Tanya frigid, were less important than the beauty of Seryozha himself which overcame her reserve.

An additional incentive for Tanya's acceptance of Seryozha's proposal is the fact that there are no other young Russian men anywhere around. Should she reject Seryozha, Tanya would have to find a non-Russian husband or accept the lonely life of a spinster. That she does accept him means a melioration of the incontrovertible isolation that has been a fact of her life.

In a rather long introduction to the novel Benson gives a complete historical, demographic, and linguistic account of the area and the people of Manchuria and Korea. She assures the reader that the problems with language—which require a Russian and a Chinese to communicate in English, which leave Koreans misunderstood in their own country, and which reduce Chinese to writing to each other because their respective dialects are unintelligible—do in fact exist. The historical accuracy of the confusion of tongues reinforces its strength as a symbol of the essential loneliness of the individuals isolated within themselves by their individual limitations.

The limitations are not simply linguistic. As men grow and become aware of new ideas they may easily become exiles in their own lands. For instance, Wilfred Chew is a Chinese who has lost his Chinese name, his Chinese religion, and the possibility of a comfortable and contented life as a bureaucrat in China. He has accepted English religion and been educated to English law in London, but must somehow support himself in the Orient. His gold tooth, which signals his foreign nature to Englishmen and Russians alike, gleams when he relives his experiences while studying law in London. But even that pleasurable time was a lonely one. Now returned to his native land, he seems well on the way to becoming an itinerant English-speaking guide for travellers in Asia.

Poor Wilfred, everywhere a foreigner with too much to say, living either with people who could not understand his speech or with people who did not want to, might be said to be the one lonely resident of a spiritual city of Babel. Not only was his world afflicted with a hopeless confusion of tongues, but also, the towers of elaborate talk he built, though always designed to reach heaven, only attained a level high enough to give him a depressing view of his audience scattering abroad beyond recall. (*TT*, 90).

Wilfred eagerly praises his acquired culture and religion which ensure his alienation in his own land; his gold tooth and goodness estranged him from the worldly citizens of England. His predicament is humorous but just below the laugh is the flutter of pity which the reader cannot ever suppress when reading a Benson novel.

Wilfred Chew is comic and pitiful; his isolation is permanent in spite of all his best efforts to break down the barriers that surround him. Yet not all the characters are so stranded. *Tobit Transplanted* offers an affirmation of life and experience, a recognition of the necessity for change, growth, and sharing in the face of the certain knowledge that all sharing will be imperfect, no gain will be without a price. This is the first of Benson's novels in which there is a fundamental change, a growth within her characters.

Both of the young people in the novel come to an understanding of themselves and the world around them that is different from that with which they began. Seryozha had "an extravagant respect for life; unconsciously, he enshrined it as a holiness. The power of movement, the sight of movement, and the feeling of movement were his trinity." (*TT*, 142). Movement and the pure state of being, of appreciating the physical world, were his pleasures. He has spent little time in self-examination although he is conscious of the occasional discrepancy between his self-image and the Seryozha the world sees. His bride-to-be, on the other hand, enjoys a pretense of transparency, of being no more than a mind observing. Life's observer, Tanya Ostapenko seems to live through her eyes. Her father's explanation for her behavior is that "she just feels far away from physical realities" (*TT*, 208). Like most of Benson's heroines, Tanya is a young woman with no strong sense of her personal identity in the world around her. "She could not see herself or put herself into words, but in her mind's eye a pillar of nothingness reared—a white mirror, passively accepting the image of hills and valleys, insect and lovers" (*TT*, 57–58). Fleeting impressions of hills, valleys, and insects are welcomed. Even impersonal pain is a source of wonder. A burned finger she presses and squeezes to make the pain more intense; fascinated, she worries the burn making the sore worse. She consciously encourages physical sensation. Yet a fiancé's touch, a kiss, has been unendurable. Lovers, because they may wish to make a more lasting impression than hills or insects, have not been welcome intruders in Tanya's world. Fiercely virgin and hostile to physical contact with demanding humans, she is relieved when her seventh engagement is broken: "The blank page of herself was safe from inscription now. She flapped a wet garment with wild joy in the air" (*TT*, 58). This image, "the blank page of herself," goes beyond a simple assertion that women must depend upon men to establish their social position. It explicitly recognizes the enormous influence of men on a woman's personal sense of identity. The role of wife or lover brings responsibilities largely absent from the duties of a daughter. As a daughter Tanya may be passive and unseen—womanly virtues. But as a wife she must be unobtrusively supportive of her husband; she must recognize and compensate for his weaknesses and vulnerabilities.

Responsibility, a husband, these have no glamour for Tanya. She would prefer to remain inviolate, alive and part of the world but with no special responsibility or understanding with another human. She has always "valued things for their independence of herself, for their incomprehensibility, for their magical remoteness" (*TT*, 129). Before Seryozha's arrival she wonders at the insistence of young men "that two *me's* could be kneaded together into an *us*":

Containers of uneasy blood—that's all we are—big and little—male and female—two-legged—many-legged—winged and creeping—wise and foolish—we slide and stride and wriggle about the earth until something called death lets the blood out, to be soaked into the ground, to be dried into the air, to form again in other containers. . . . Why should there be any of this merging between one skin-full of blood and bones and another—why can't we get used to the loneliness of having separate blood? Pitchers may go to the same well, be dipped, and come home full, clinking handles, tinkling together—but always separate—each with its dreadful integrity complete—its inviolate solitary storm of contents. Not till the pitcher is spilled is there a merging into thirsty space. (*TT*, 121).

The image of the pitchers is particularly appropriate for Tanya's sense of the world and herself because it reveals the extent of her perceived passivity. Containers clink and tinkle when acted upon, left to themselves they stand quietly. Until the night when she chooses to marry Seryozha, Tanya has chosen to remain inactive. Tanya's mother is aware of the paucity of this passivity. Herself unable to respond to physical closeness, she can hope that the imprisoning isolation of her daughter can be shattered. Contemplating the dreaded moment of her daughter's wedding night, Varvara Ostapenko recognizes that "she was seeing a vision of the breaking of dear loneliness, the breaking of the virgin round world by the forces of fire and water and wind, the breaking open of strong remote mountains, breaking into chasms and seas, craters, valleys and peaks . . . a world the richer for its broken integrity—its lost virginity. To make a statue was to break a stone. Being alive was a breaking of death. To become something was to shatter the peace of being nothing" (*TT*, 222). To see the world as it is one must not only contemplate the distant, cool, virginal mountains but also appreciate the varied nearer landscape: jagged, pocked, but clothed with flowers. Varvara Ostapenko, who has only imperfectly escaped the virginal isolation, recognizes the inadequacy of the virginal experience for full life.

Tanya's sense of detachment from the world around her is stressed, but her isolation does not have the morbid emphasis given in earlier books. The color gray, pervasive in *I Pose*, *Living Alone*, and *Goodbye, Stranger*, is almost entirely absent. Tanya's skirt is a faded light blue, but her auburn hair suggests the vibrant life within her. That life blossoms forth because she chooses life.

The central scene of the novel is a highly comic one, but the comedy in no way detracts from the importance of the details of the scene, details which stress the fact that Tanya has *decided*, not simply accepted. The English-trained Chinese lawyer's contract for a marriage between Russians in Korea is a parody of a sales contract, but Benson makes it quite clear that Tanya has not been sold but has chosen to wed. Admittedly, there was psychological pressure (as well as the presumed benefit of the smell of rotting fish organs being burned) to induce her to accept the proposal. But Tanya chooses. Her mother, dreading her daughter's wedding night, insists that Seryozha not go to her room but instead brings Tanya out to the kitchen to talk to him. Thus, the young people are left alone to decide for themselves what they will do, and it is clear that Tanya has chosen to accept the young man. They retire quietly together to her room.

The morning Seryozha rises a married man he feels that his old innocent self is a thing of the past. "For the first time in his life, Seryozha was shaken—shaken in his stalwart anonymity—called home to self-consciousness by a sort of earthquake of the heart. He had been invisible, he had been a matter of course, he had been too close to see . . . Now this earthquake intrusion of a trespasser had shaken him awake—had forced him to turn and meet himself" (*TT*, 231–32). Seryozha's marriage unearths a new and acute self-consciousness. It introduces Seryozha to introspection and stirs faint suspicions of the possibility of vague inadequacies within himself.

Tanya also soon recognizes her loss of anonymity with the acceptance of a husband. As she approaches the breakfast table with her husband she suddenly feels "Vulnerably visible herself—she who had been unconscious—bodiless—invisible all her life. . . . It was as though the old story of the magic cloak of invisibility had been reversed; by wrapping her water-clear impersonality in this wide cloak of reality that Seryozha was, she was seen—seen—a woman at last—obliged to offer herself for acceptance or rejection by the eyes of strangers—obliged to ask humbly for tolerance, from eyes" (*TT*, 244). Close on the heels of Tanya's new self-consciousness and sense of vulnerability is a new protective affection. Watching her new husband move around the room, she recognizes his vulnerability and silently supports him. Identifying with Seryozha, Tanya feels "as if she were with him inside his too-visible body which quailed, yet hoped for the best—which preened itself yet feared rebuff. She felt herself the true traditional wife—helping him to strengthen his ramparts—arming and encouraging the tender *I* inside that tough body" (*TT*, 245). Tanya understands without explicit instruction that a wife's responsibility is more than passive loyalty. She must consciously, if not overtly, defend her husband's vulnerabilities.

This support beginning in Tanya has matured in both Anna and Varvara. The older Malinins and the Ostapenkos are couples united by habit and pity, and the pity nurtures affection and manifestations of tenderness. Significantly, the men in these marriages seem in greater need of protection than their wives do.

Old Sergei, a failed businessman who is providentially removed from responsibility for his family's fading fortunes by the onset of his blindness, is a thin pathetic creature whose main joy seems to be contrived sorrow. Meditations upon death, orphans and widows, and helpless living things produce in him a "limp ecstasy" (*TT*, 38). This pleasurable morbidity is his goal when he is not busy posing as a Husband with a Righteous Grievance, or a Man of Great Business Affairs. Dependent upon his wife and son, he nonetheless treats the son as a child and is querulous and complaining with his wife. Nearly helpless and usually annoying, Old Sergei is an irritating background noise with which his wife must contend. Yet he is essential to her. His pathetic figure and condition inspire Anna with a pity that softens her irritation, brings him unexpected tendernesses, and allows her a sense of importance.

Anna Malinin is a large, spontaneous woman who believes "she had been endowed with a superfluity of power to hurt and thwart people" (*TT*, 74). Widely embracing life and devoted to her son, she is often plagued by remorse for usually harmless statements which she perceives in retrospect as in some way offensive to other people. Caring for her husband, she often showers him with unexpected kindnesses. The small acts of thoughtfulness are generally inspired by guilt and offered as atonement for slights both real and imagined. Fat Anna, who was slim and educated when she married her husband because she thought he was wise, recognizes that if he had been as wise as she had thought, he would not have married her and she would be a solitary woman. So this couple, long removed from passion, continues in mutual dependence: Sergei needing the practical aid of his wife, and Anna, needing to be needed.

Tanya's family presents a similar picture of isolation and mutual dependence. Varvara Ostapenko, accepting the idea that there is a serious incompleteness in her own character, embraces and supports the expansive though weak personality of her husband Pavel. Pavel, who believes words can create reality, talks until the words seem to be arranged in such a perfect order that the validity of their meaning has to be accepted. Empty of perceived truth, he creates his own truth. His wife often admonishes him to *think*. She hopes that he will compare his verbal creations with the facts from which his ideas are supposed to have sprung. But Pavel can only pause in the creation of his towers of words. Varvara, recognizing her husband's weaknesses, mentally transforms those weaknesses into eccentricities, then defends them as unique features of a personality well worth admiring. This consciousness of weakness combined with a refusal to admit the weaknesses creates a situation in which all members of the Ostapenko family harbor "a chronic soreness of heart. They all almost hated and quite loved one another—savage in their disappointment of their own hopes one of another, and savage in their anger against outsiders for being disappointed" (*TT*, 114).

Defending each other's weaknesses against the attack of outsiders, Varvara and Pavel are not able to aid each other in effecting changes in what may be perceived as imperfections of character.

The participants in these two marriages are revealed in some of their limitations, and the disappointments the partners receive from each other are carefully suggested. The reader does not think that either marriage was a mistake, that any of the four could or should be better situated. In *This Is the End* the reader wishes Mr. Russell could have a wife in England instead of one who works for peace in the United States (which was not at the time at war). In *Living Alone* the reader might wish Pinehurst could have introduced his wife, Lady Arabel Higgins, to his magic propensities so that she could have better loved and understood her husband and her son. The reader of *The Poor Man* might wonder if Tam McTab might have become more than superficial and egocentric if he had had the courage to marry not an assenting listener but an unpredictable, sharp-minded challenger. There are no such wishes and speculations from the reader of *Tobit Transplanted*. The novel discloses the way things are, and the reader may feel a certain relief that things are no worse.

It is, after all, the unconscious ability to evoke pity that wins for the characters in this novel a modicum of affection from those who surround them. Seryozha is first attracted to Tanya when he notices "the day-worn look of the hem of her skirt, the dust on her blunt Chinese shoes, [which] humbled her charmingly in his sight" (*TT*, 139). Tanya, on the other hand, is drawn to Seryozha when she watches him shyly trying to be the man he believes he should be with her father. Even Anna, generous-hearted mother of Seryozha, who has heard her daughter-in-law described as Death, warms to the girl when she discovers she can pity her: "'Presently,' thought Anna, 'she'll be horrified to remember that she said that.' And instantly she felt at ease with Tanya" (*TT*, 327). Tanya, evading Anna's touch and realizing the action may hurt her mother-in-law's feelings, smiles "a bewildered and compassionate smile . . . having withdrawn herself, she felt tender" and exerts herself to try to put Anna at ease (*TT*, 328). Pity is the mortar of all unions. Pavel Ostapenko is pitied by his wife, who tries to protect him from the disapproval of outsiders; some part of Pavel's attitude toward his wife, with her incomplete nature and vivid red birthmark on her cheek, must be pity—a feeling which would fit well with his self-important posture. Anna's pity for Sergei not only prompts her to care for him, but also to try to be kind. Even the whining Sergei is moved to pity, and in his blindness tries to comfort Anna when she fears for the safety of their son.

Indispensable to the success of all of Benson's novels has been the wit and humor with which she treats even the most serious subjects. With few exceptions, most of the humor in her novels is derived from the ironic commentary of the narrator. In *Tobit Transplanted*, however, irony gives way to outright comedy in the central scene of the novel. Wilfred Chew, unable to understand a word of the conversation which is being conducted in Russian, draws up a marriage agreement while for the first time under the influence of champagne. Not admitting even to himself that he suspects the contract might not be absolutely correct, Pavel Ostapenko urges a virtual stranger toward his daughter's bedroom in order to have her conform to what he thinks grown daughters should be: married. The comic tension of the entire evening builds toward and is maintained after the moment when the young couple leave to consummate their marriage—a consummation which Tanya's father soon becomes convinced will bring instant death to the bridegroom. But the comedy in no way disguises the important points that it envelops. The most important point, of course, is that Tanya does choose to marry, and her marriage is not the defeat that it was for Jay in *This Is the End* or would have been for Ipsie in *Pipers and a Dancer*. Marriage for Tanya becomes a sharing. Growing from a comic, drunken dinner, her commitment is more binding than the worthless though socially accurate contract she signs. And this is the second point: neither priest nor legal document is more important than personal commitment. Neither law nor religion could bind her more securely to Seryozha than she herself chooses to be bound.

It is perhaps belaboring the obvious to point out that a reader's perception of comedy, irony, pathos or tragedy is dependent upon a standard against which the reader may measure events. This self-evident fact must be recognized if any of Benson's work is to be properly appreciated. Benson always strives to puncture easy answers, and nowhere is this more apparent than in *Tobit Transplanted*. A final illustration of this phenomenon: The morning after their marriage Seryozha and Tanya watch the birth of a foal and are thrilled as they watch the emergence of new life. The narrator observes, "*Living* was that things *were*, after all—living—and nothing else, really. In this these two contrary lovers agree, sinking their contrariness—they agreed to let things live—let things be. This *being* was the Unknown God, to whom both, obscurely, owed homage—this exquisite inhumanity—immorality—impudence—oblivion—urgency—this tremendous relevance called life. To the admission *It Is*, nothing is irrelevant except *It Ought To Be*" (*TT*, 305). One might at first agree with Tanya and Seryozha that "to the admission *It Is*, nothing is irrelavant except *It Ought To Be*." But finishing the novel, the reader realizes that the recognition that situations are not as they ought to be can create comedy. Furthermore, the compassion springing from the wish that what *is* were not so vulnerable is what creates the *us* from separate containers of uneasy blood. The divergence of opinion of what ought to be permits greater opportunity for weak vessels to receive reinforcement from pitying companion containers.

Chapter Seven
Arrangements and Collections
Pull Devil, Pull Baker
and *Collected Short Stories*

Before their publication in the posthumous *Collected Short Stories* (1936), quite a few of Benson's short stories had appeared before the public at least twice. They would appear first in magazines, then be issued in small, limited editions. There were in all four of these small collections: *The Awakening* (1925), *The Man Who Missed the Bus* (1928), *Hope Against Hope and Other Stories* (1931), and *Christmas Formula and Other Stories* (1932). More than a collection but not exactly a novel is *Pull Devil, Pull Baker*, published in 1933.

In her introduction to *Pull Devil, Pull Baker* Benson explains that she is acting as editor for autobiographical "Love Stories of My" written by Count Nicolas De Toulouse Lautrec De Savine, K. M., an old man in a hospital ward in Hong Kong. He describes himself as "a very good-known men, who belong to one of the most distinguished aristocratic famelys of Europe—pretty wellknown all the world other."[1] His stories, recorded in his own English and his own spelling, are told with the amoral innocence of the utterly self-centered. To the "moral confectionery" of his baker, the devil, in the guise of the editor Stella Benson, contrasts tales stripped of sentimentality and bathetic indulgence. For instance, a story of the Count's youth includes a minor episode with a tailor. The episode is supposed to demonstrate the heartlessness and greed of Jews when an evening of profitable gambling is interrupted by the Count's Jewish tailor who tries to collect the money owed him. The pathetic tailor explains that his wife and three children are ill and he must have the money due him, a sum which is a small fraction of the amount piled in front of the Count. Instead of receiving the money, the tailor is shot at. The sound of the shot frightens the man into a faint; when he is revived he finds the young gambler still determined not to pay him. The tailor is thrown out, the evening finishes with a flourish, and the story continues with further adventures for the Count. The Count's grand story is followed by the editor's addition—the tailor's version of the episode. Instead of developing the pathos of a poor man with a sick family, the story exposes a man who accepts humiliation without ever considering that it should not be his natural experience. Neither his wife nor his one child is ill. The tailor himself has a head cold, but his world-weariness leaves him indifferent to his own discomfort. Eschewing the quick easy bid for sympathy, Benson develops a character eliciting a far greater compassion than would be accorded for a mere illness in the family. When the tailor believes he is dead, he rejoices in the peace of death. His anguish upon discovering that he is still alive and so must endure further humiliation moves the reader to a genuine and lasting pity. The tailor's undramatic, quiet despair, his world-weariness, seem much more real than the Count's extravagant adventures.

In fact, the adventures might well have been transformed with the passing of time. One of the Count's tales of daring escape and brilliant brazenness is told from the safe distance of forty years, then contrasted with a more probable version of the events as they actually befell. The devil remembers the unromantic exhaustion and the childish appeal for help; the Count remembers his calm nerve as he interrupts a party attended by judges, attorneys, and gendarmerie captains. The effect of the juxtaposition of the stories is to remind the reader that the sharp design of reality can be transformed by time into the soft patina of romance.

Similarly, the Count's two loving stories, "Angelina" and "Lili, the Noty Gerl," are juxtaposed with the story of "The Man Who Fell in Love with the Cooperative Stores." The result is a criticism of the self-indulgence that permits a Don Juan of Our Day to feel aggrieved when a mistress, originally captivated by lavish spending, departs with a wealthier lover. The Count's headlong excitement and unreflective selfishness in the telling of the tale almost win him sympathy for his misadventures with "crooky" females. But "The Man Who Fell in Love with the Cooperative Stores" adds the summary comment to the Count's romantic adventures: "Surely it stands to reason that anything that money can buy once, money can buy again" (*PD, PB*, 193). As counterpoint to the Count's loving stories, "The Man Who Fell in Love with the Cooperative Stores" works quite well. A young man interpreting store advertisements as romantic invitations and bills as love letters seems not so ridiculous when compared to men buying the attention of young attractive women and interpreting the purchased attention as spontaneous affection.

In the final analysis *Pull Devil, Pull Baker* is closer to an arrangement of short stories than to a novel. By the arrangement the stories lend each other support and become stronger. "The Man Who Fell in Love with the Cooperative Stores" succeeds in *Pull Devil, Pull Baker* but is quite weak when standing alone in *Collected Short Stories*. The story taken by itself seems to be the kind of attack on materialism that sounds good when first conceived but is too outrageous to be effective. The language conforms precisely to what is expected of the lovelorn. The story is of a man in love with a store—not with buying or the process of acquisition but with the store itself. The analogy to the business of love sounds good, but it does not quite work. Although the story demonstrates well the narrator's concluding observations and the tone of the parody of the love lament is well maintained, the elements do not cohere as an imaginative whole which wins the emotional assent of the reader. It is the sort of idea that Benson's detractors might term "too cute." However, when placed beside the cream puffery of the Count in *Pull Devil, Pull Baker*, its literal preposterousness fades rather quickly as the reader automatically compares the situation in the love stories.

The opposite malady afflicts another of the stories in *Collected Short Stories*. "A Dream" powerfully evokes a nightmare world of desolation punctured by a distant clanging. But having entered so completely the experience of a woman with a brain tumor, the reader is disappointed with the ending. Benson began the story with the explanation that it is the transcription of a dream, but as she had observed elsewhere, other people's dreams seem pointless. The reader's disappointment springs from the fact that he has *felt* the dream, but the flat ending diminishes the entire experience. What *is*, after all, the point of sharing a dream? Dreams, of course, have the annoying habit of having inexplicable details, but readers have the equally annoying habit of searching for the significance of, if not the explanation for, the inexplicable. Alas, reader and writer are at cross purposes here. When the woman wanders over a hill in the wasteland she finds her old nurse Zillah. Zillah is loving and friendly but uneasy. The uneasiness serves only to produce an anticlimax. The reader knows long before Zillah's announcement that both women are dead; the unease has given it away. But *why* is Zillah uneasy? Surely not because she has to break the news of death! There must be more to it.

Stella Benson's short stories are very uneven in quality. Most do give a strong sense of a story told; there is a completeness about them that is not always present in this form which lends itself so readily to recounting incident with no sense of finality. However, although a few stories don't quite come off, most are good and four are extremely good.

"Hope Against Hope" is a moving attack on conventional attitudes toward women. The limited omniscience in the third-person point of view is restricted to the thoughts and actions of the convalescing man who is attended in his recovery by a plain but pleasant, and as it turns out imaginative and lonely, nurse. In spite of her patience with him, her unfailing good humor, and her professional attentiveness, Ward Clark "felt justified in despising her, since he thought of himself as a reasonable-looking and still-young man, in spite of the fact that he was older than she was, that his nose was a little crooked, and that baldness ran up like a boulevard to the crown of his head between two thinned thickets of fair curly hair. Still, he felt himself a man—what a man ought to be—and knew her to be absurdly faded and virgin—exactly what a woman ought not to be."[2] Miss Hope has committed the unpardonable sin of being an unmarried female over the age of thirty. Throughout the story thirty-six year old Ward Clark is disgusted by Miss Hope's enjoyment of conversation with a fifty-year old schoolteacher who has an annoying sniff. While Clark is being rude to and contemptuous of Miss Hope, he is basking in the light of the schoolteacher's daughter's infatuation. This nineteen-year old girl finds Clark extremely attractive, his age enhances his romance in her innocent eyes. The story ends with Clark, utterly incredulous that Miss Hope has attempted suicide, sending her away. Clark will send for his sister to come care for him (she is a woman and therefore will have no other duty apparently!); he neither inquires into nor cares about the reason for the suicide attempt.

Since the focus is on the man's perceptions, the reader sees his irritation with every suggestion, however unconscious, that Miss Hope is a person. He prefers to consider her a dull background whose conscientious pleasantries deserve no more than rudeness. It never crosses his mind that she could be interesting for herself, or that any man might find her so. Ward accepts as his due, on the other hand, the empty-headed adoration of a nineteen-year old girl. The story not only exposes a double standard—an expectation that women must remain pure, and a contempt for those who do—but also criticizes society's treatment of unmarried women who are no longer young. To accomplish this Benson insists upon the ordinariness of Miss Hope. Like Clark, the reader sees her as a bit ridiculous in her humble vanities. Therefore, the shock of surprise is especially sharp at the realization that her capacity for love has been completely ignored. The reader has been guilty of the same prejudice—perhaps in a milder form—that Ward Clark has.

"Submarine" is a mood piece, conveying quite effectively the growing terror in a woman's mind as guilt for an earlier heartlessness rises to haunt her. The action of the story is beneath the surface of the ocean as a couple go diving. Their air hoses are controlled by a man who the wife becomes convinced is the son of her former nana. The nana had been with the wife for twenty years, but when the new husband suspected that she had embezzled money, he fired her instantly. Beneath the surface of the water long-submerged guilt floats back to the wife. Regretting that she had not defended her nana, that she had not opposed her husband's will, the wife becomes convinced that the man controlling their air lines intends to exact vengeance by drowning them for the injury done years ago to his mother. Her mounting panic is played against the incongruity of the appearance of her husband. Looking like a rhinoceros in his diving suit, the man bumbles about like a clown. When they are finally safe again above water the reader understands from the final lines that the wife feels not just guilt but also resentment: resentment toward her husband who so completely changed her life years ago by assuming control of her household, who had been so oblivious to her recent heart-stopping terror. Safe on the boat, the wife looks at her husband "as the raftman helpfully wrenched his iron head off" (*CSS*, 87).

One of the best of all Benson's short stories, "The Desert Islander" pits the determined individualist against the ingrained organization man. The antagonists are a Russian deserter from the Foreign Legion in China and an Englishman from whom he seeks assistance. The deserter insists upon being an individual, a unique individual. He bristles whenever compared to anyone else or considered as part of any group. It is his article of faith that anything he does, because he does it, must be original and therefore good. The Englishman, on the other hand, does always what he should. At the risk (indeed finally at the cost) of his life he behaves decently. Because the Russian's infected leg must receive medical attention, the Englishman drives him through a war to get help. The recipient of the automatic assistance, far from being grateful, grows to hate his benefactor because he has seen too much of the deserter's fears and weakness for the Russian soldier to maintain his self-image as a fearless individualist. The deserter's attitude is understandable, in fact it may be typical of the twentieth century, but it is also willfully foolish and even selfishly cruel. The Russian would rather produce a meaningless cacophony than listen to someone else's music. He would rather see the man who saved his life dead than know that somewhere someone had seen his own terror and helplessness. The Englishman has opposite inclinations. Automatically accepting the duty to aid the injured, he takes risks for a stranger that many men would not dare for themselves. In the midst of war and mud he is impeccably dressed. But his life is senselessly taken by a stray bullet as he waves goodbye to a man who despises him. The individualist survives but the world seems no better for the loss of the convention-loving man.

"Story Coldly Told" addresses more broadly the weakness of unexamined conventions. The title suggests detachment, and detachment suggests an absence of caring. But while criticizing sentimental caring, the story itself demonstrates that there is something in the world other than reason. The narrator, Palmer, lives in an isolated city in an out-of-the-way country and is the last representative of a dying commercial activity. He seems mildly interested in the goings-on around him but personally uninvolved. Even his sense of identity is ambiguous as he describes himself "like the blessed Damosel" watching a scene below him. Few men would liken themselves to the image of a woman, no matter what the circumstance. A native who works for him, but for whom he feels no sense of friendship, rescues Palmer, an English vice-consul, and a seventy-five year old woman missionary from revolutionaries by turning the three of them over to a band of brigands.

During their captivity the vice-consul, who had been full of admiration for the noble savages among whom he lived, is insulted by them and comes to fear them. The missionary, who has lived in the country for thirty-five years without ever bothering to learn anything about its culture, preaches love to men who believe she is a eunuch dedicated to a special god. The first sign that her missionary efforts are effective is the return of a stolen sweater. The next sign comes from the leader of the band who tells Palmer that if the woman doesn't stop talking he will cut out her tongue—several of his men have abandoned their life of crimes because of her. Before the resolve of the leader can be tested, a rescue party arrives. As the party approaches, three of the brigands offer final proof of Miss Sims's effectiveness. They murder their leader in front of everyone. This murder is supposed to demonstrate the sincerity of their newfound faith in the religion of love; with the killing they reject their sinful past. No one—not Miss Sims who preaches love, nor the vice-consul who admires the natural nobility of savages, nor the men who had followed Rak Mandi—seems to regret his death. No one, that is, except the narrator. Palmer, who has associated neither with his captors nor his fellow prisoners, who does not "believe in pretty communications between man and man—least of all between white man and negro," (*CSS*, 303), regrets the passing of a life that seemed to have had a sense of direction. Palmer, who believes he lives without sentimentality, is the only person to try to make the dying man's last moments comfortable.

This story of misunderstanding and death ends on a quietly positive note. In spite of sentimental blindness (the vice-consul's belief in idealized noble savages instead of living people), fanatic ignorance (Miss Sims's lack of interest in the realities of the world around her), and religious misunderstanding (the converts' murder of their leader in the name of the religion offered by what they believe is a eunuch), communion is possible. A man who cultivates detachment respects the integrity of life and can be moved, against all reason, to a gesture of brotherhood through an act of impractical sympathy. It is the possibility of sympathy through an unsentimental respect for life that Benson's entire work insists upon.

Poems

Poems was published in 1935, a collection of poems which Benson herself had selected before her death. Most had appeared before, either in the 1918 volume *Twenty* or in one of her first six novels. Benson's poems do not cover a wide range of subjects or styles, but they do glow with a quiet loveliness. Yearning for belief, resolute in isolation, glorying in beauty, they speak for the lonely who have felt life's splendor. Whereas in her novels and travel articles Benson never strays far from the light touch, in her poetry she exposes emotion without the protective covering of humor or playful irony. What irony there is compresses the pain of empathy, as in "To Him That Hath. . . . ":

> You who have Mary for kin
> And Jesus for friend,
> Pray for a sinless
> Heart unendingly.
> And to you who are blind with tears
> Your good God sends
> The heartrending
> Fellowship of sufferers.

This naked pain is usually more hidden in her prose works.

Benson does tend to an elevated diction and occasional archaisms which obscure meaning. For instance, in "Christmas, 1917" the use of the archaic "holden" seems to have nothing to speak for it other than that it rhymes with "golden"—and everything going against it including the fact that it does not make much sense in the stanza. In the next stanza "stonèd" is rhymed with "enthronèd," but why the extra syllable in each word? But these are her worst offenses. In a collection revealing so honestly a sense of isolation and betrayal in the world, there are precious few slips into sentimentality. More typical is the hauntingly lovely "The Cornishman."

> At sunset, when the high sea span
> About the rocks a web of foam,
> I saw the ghost of a Cornishman
> Come home.
> I saw the ghost of a Cornishman
> Run from the weariness of war,
> I heard him laughing as he ran
> Across his unforgotten shore.
> The great cliff, gilded by the west,
> Received him as an honoured guest.
> The green sea, shining in the bay,
> Did drown his dreadful yesterday.
>
> Come home, come home, you million ghosts,
> The honest years shall make amends,
> The sun and moon shall be your hosts,
> The everlasting hills your friends.
> And some shall seek their mothers' faces,
> And some shall run to trysting-places,
> And some to towns, and others yet
> Shall find great forests in their debt.
> Oh, I would siege the golden coasts
> Of space, and climb high heaven's dome,
> So I might see those million ghosts
> Come home.

Travel Articles

Many of Benson's travel articles are collected in two books. The first, *The Little World* (1925), includes pieces written between 1919 and 1924 during travels in the United States, China, and India. *Worlds Within Worlds* (1928) reflects an appreciation for the humor and beauty of the world through close observation of the details of the life around her. Observations made when she was feeling particularly unsympathetic to the missionaries, French officials, and Chinese who surrounded her offer an excellent tonic for the reader who is satiated with accounts of the "Mystic Withdrawn Orient, Shot with the Glances of Dark Almond

Eyes that See Beyond Mere Human Wisdon."[3] It is the human that unfailingly attracts Benson, and the human that she seeks. Her descriptions entertain and the entertainment instructs.

An evening of stylized Chinese drama inspires a comparison of Hollywood's determination to deny importance to anyone over twenty-five (small helpless infants have a particularly powerful effect upon Americans) with China's emphasis on reverence for the aged. Benson employs the child's eye view to describe outward appearance. The effect, as seen below, is that the reader has a vivid image of a Chinese play and a smile for the foibles in the variety of human tragedy.

> Chinese heart-strings are a tougher instrument to play upon than American heart-strings, and nothing more tender than a heavy widow, played by a full-sized he-man, can strike a chord of sympathy east of Suez. We had just such a widow at the Chinese theatre last night. She was tall and not too closely shaven and had a very powerful bass voice. Her sleeves were about twice as long as her arms and she used them as a handkerchief. Her white horsehair wig was built into a tall tower. When she needed to relieve her feelings by a poignant female scream of anguish, a little trumpet played by a member of the orchestra, backstage, had to do it for her. The widow's eldest son—black-hearted fellow—had found a good job in a distant place, married, and never written to his mother again. She had sent her second son to remind him of his duty. The second son also never came back—indeed how could he?— for his brother and sister-in-law drove a three-inch nail into his head and buried him hastily as soon as he arrived. And now the widow was going herself, plodding ferociously round and round the stage and shouldering her massive umbrella with an expression that boded no good for undutiful sons. The ghost of her second son met her on the road. He wore ordinary coolie clothes with the addition of a long horsetail dangling from his left ear to his knee. His nose was painted white, with a little black spot on the bridge to show where the three-inch nail went in. When his mother saw him—toot-toot-toot—the little trumpet expressed her feelings for her, she tossed her umbrella over her shoulder and did a farcical backward somersault. That's the worst of Chinese plays—you never know when you can safely cry. (*WWW*, 193)

And that is the worst—the best—of Stella Benson as well. The reader often knows that tears are called for if he is to live by the rules of convention and sentiment. But Benson will not allow such quick escape. A retreat to easy emotion allows the incident to be enjoyed and placed. Benson interweaves the humor and sadness of mortality with the beauty of a living response. After all, if the Orient is inscrutible, then one need not consider the people within it, there is no point of identification. Above all, common life unites us. For instance, the recognition that lovely painted Japanese geishas are also women prompts Benson's observations that "I cannot help feeling glad that when my soul was, in the beginning, classified as female and given to an underling angel to be disposed of on earth, it was not fitted with a Japanese body. I cannot think that there would be very much left of that soul by now."[4] Japan becomes more real for the poignant reflection on the individual women behind their white powder and their butterfly-like solicitude for the pleasure of Japanese men.

In some moods Benson can treat hostilities between Japan and China or the civil war in China lightheartedly; she makes men sound like children squabbling. But this tone is not indicative of callous indifference to human suffering. A description of a trip up a river can encompass criticism of war by calling quiet attention to the human cost of war—any war.

> There was war in Szechuan—if you could call it war, for there were no posters about war. No pictures of strapping heroes encouraged those who felt neither strapping nor heroic to find out what tonic war could do for them. In Szechuan war advertised itself; one saw the war and one saw the heroes—which was unfortunate from the point of view of those who deal in war. Even the losers advertised the war. I watched the dead losers go, in procession but not in triumph, face downward down the river, threading their forlorn way through the plaited rapids, pausing indifferently in the quiet reaches where the water enfolded them like gold silk. I saw the less fortunate losers come to seek the protection of the mountains, the wounded slung painfully on poles carried by unfriendly coolies forced into service, or riding on bleeding and dying ponies. (*LW*, 86-87)

But Benson's concern about physical death is transitory. She returns over and over again to incidents that suggest the failure of intellectual communication, while the very success of her imagery nurtures the sympathetic communication between individuals that she found so often lacking. For example, in a Korean train she accidentally dropped a cigarette down the padded back of a Korean's coat. Alas, she was unable to make the man understand his problem. With no common language she resorted to trying a charade to point out his danger. However, since she was not only a foreigner but a woman as well, her audience decided to ignore her before perplexity could change to annoyance. The serious consequences of the smoldering cigarette are overshadowed in the amusing final scene of a man walking off unaware of the thin wisp of smoke rising behind his neck. With no explicit generalization, Benson adds one more tile to the mosaic of her enduring theme. Isolated man may be, and inconsequential to others, yet there is grandeur as man, determinedly blind to the potential pain always with him, goes on with the business of living.

Stella Benson's travel articles can bear comparison to any of the best, to those of Rebecca West or Graham Greene. She always gives the reader the feeling of immediate participation in vivid experience. Perhaps more important, she manages to make the exotic believable. While comparing the strange with the familiar, she encourages an appreciation of the beauty and variety of life and universal individuality, and thus opens the reader's eyes anew to the familiar world around him.

Chapter Eight
Conclusion

Stella Benson believed her conscious identity more significant than her biological identity—that she was a writer was more significant than the fact that she was a woman—as a writer, not a woman writer, she should be judged. And it was as a writer that David Daiches judged her in 1958. He described Stella Benson as "a highly original novelist whose tragic view of life is artfully disposed behind a facade of remarkable comic wit."[1] Benson recognized the difficulty of bringing to term the joy latent in life, and her work recognizes the frequent failure of the imagination, but she never lost sight of the continuing presence of potential. Her wit and imagination contradict the intellectual message of tragedy in the factual world.

Tobit Transplanted is a clear descendent of *I Pose* and *The Poor Man*. These three novels seem to anchor themselves firmly in the real world. All three suggest that there is an external world of verifiable fact by which we must judge ourselves. All three have central characters with clear objectives and practical activities in the external world. The suffragette in *I Pose*, unmarried by chance, has dedicated herself to achieving something more than what society has allotted her. She wants to consider the situation in the world around her and improve the lot of women. Emily in *The Poor Man* seeks emotional fulfillment with a married man and has travelled as his secretary to accomplish her objective. Tanya in *Tobit Transplanted* has sought to avoid emotional responsibility by maintaining her status as daughter. Each of the three women must adjust either her objective or her activities.

Faced with conflicting desires, the suffragette chooses to give up the need for choice. Although she wants the comfort of a husband she will not narrow her vision to include only domestic life. Drawn toward marriage by desire though not by choice, she elects to remove herself completely from a world in which she cannot reconcile conflicting roles. Emily in *The Poor Man* refuses to settle for any man just because he is a man. Faced with loneliness and the certain knowledge that her affair with Tam is over, she nonetheless chooses to be alone rather than accept Edward Williams as a lover. She exercises a positive choice which does not bring immediate happiness but allows her the dignity of independent action. Finally, Tanya, as she realizes that her desire for freedom from responsibility will be thwarted by her father's insistence that she become what he believes she should be, chooses another sort of invisibility when attracted to a man who seems to share her respect for life. Although she takes on the responsibility of a husband and the emotional support that requires she will gain a new kind of transparency. She will fulfill the expected role of wife and will be freed from criticism of her "unnatural" nature. These three novels all deal with women who have an idea of what they are and what they want, and the novels follow the women as they do or do not attain their objectives. These novels are fundamentally traditional in conception and development. There is a romantic interest, there is a male protagonist of importance at least equal to—and in the case of *The Poor Man* greater than—that of the female central character. Even *I Pose*, with its feminist bent, its unnamed protagonists, and its dramatic rejection of marriage is far more traditional in tone and perspective than *This Is the End* with its nearly conventional ending or *Pipers and a Dancer* with its absence of any hint of magic.

Tobit Transplanted offers depth of characterization and greater realism than *I Pose*, but the singular accomplishment of that first novel should not be overlooked. *I Pose* makes a clear and unambiguous statement about the frustration and actual hardship suffered by women imprisoned by stereotypes and self-serving masculine prejudice. Serving strictly moral ends *I Pose* is armed with witticisms shooting truths home to an enchanted reader.

As the narrator of *I Pose* points out, "Imagination seems to be a glory and a misery, a blessing and a curse. Adam, to his sorrow, lacked it. Eve, to her sorrow, possessed it. Had both been blessed—or cursed—with it, there would have been much keener competition for the apple" (*IP*, 4). It is the glory and the misery of the imagination that Benson demonstrates in *This Is the End*, *Living Alone*, *Pipers and a Dancer*, and *Goodbye, Stranger*. Most reviewers appreciating these books comment on the wit and the feeling of magic in them. What has not been sufficiently stressed is the fact that their real power comes from the clear creation of a tangible reality against which the insubstantial world of the imagination wavers. Benson focuses the reader's eyes not on great numbers of details but on significant detail, and creates a strong, realistic impression of the external world in which her characters must cope. As the reader works to bring this world of the imagination into focus, he shares the frustration of the women ill at ease in their situations. These four novels are Benson's most original accomplishments. They all develop a specifically feminine consciousness. In none of these novels does the heroine have a fixed sense of her own identity. Nor does she have a specific vision of her future, or even a clear idea of how best to handle the present. Her knowledge that there is more to her self than the world will acknowledge is her glory and her misery. Both the glory and the misery grow with increased awareness of the valuable intangibles of life.

Reginald Johnson said in response to Benson's first three novels that she was a woman writing for women. He was only partially correct. Stella Benson was a woman writing *about* women, but she was writing *to* all people prepared to try to look anew at themselves and the world around them. As it happened, Benson wrote about the isolation of women who live restricted by what society deems appropriate for them. But as women increasingly insist on the freedom to be persons, all people, men and women, are pushed toward a new freedom, a demanding freedom in which each must decide for himself or herself which possible self he or she will pursue.

Most critics have agreed that *Tobit Transplanted* is her best work, but perhaps some readers' evaluations have depended too heavily upon what they were comfortable with. With *Tobit Transplanted* many readers could enjoy in comfort a novel with a clear story line, vivid imagery, consistent characterization, friendly humor, and perceptive observation. It is, as Benson herself described it, a friendly book, and there is no doubt that it is a remarkable literary achievement. But the familiarity and safety of *Tobit Transplanted* with its positive ending has unfortunately tended to overshadow her earlier accomplishments. If *Tobit Transplanted* is lit by the bright light of the sun, Benson's other novels seem to glimmer with ethereal magic in the light of the moon. Although *Tobit Transplanted* is Stella Benson's most widely acclaimed book, it is not on that novel alone that her reputation must rest. *I Pose, Pipers and a Dancer, Goodbye, Stranger,* and *Tobit Transplanted* are all worthy results of artistic effort. Benson's exploration of isolation and defeat is developed through her understanding of the frustrating position of women. Her message, though, is not for women only. Painfully aware of life's cruelty and humanity's weakness, she sought to strengthen the soul through gaiety and to train the eye to see beauty. All the while she reminded the intellect that the world could be better.

In 1976 Martin Seymour-Smith included Stella Benson in *Who's Who in Twentieth Century Literature* although she has received virtually no

Conclusion

critical attention in four decades. He included Stella Benson while he omitted Vera Brittain, Winifred Holtby, Sheila Kaye-Smith, Rose Macaulay, May Sinclair, and Elinor Wylie: contemporaries of Stella Benson all of whom have received more recent critical attention than she has. Benson's novels are witty and haunting. Her poetry complements them in its seriousness. Her accomplishment is original and significant. Christopher Morley once said that lazy and contented people will never appreciate her work. That is probably true, but for those who dare the disarming challenge she waits to be appreciated.

Appendix

Libraries with unpublished Benson material:

BM	British Museum: Sidney Schiff (Stephen Hudson)
HL	Harvard Library:
	Witter Bynner
	Amy Lowell
LC:	Library of Congress: Albert Bender
MC:	Mills College Library: Albert Bender
NYP-B	New York Public Library, Berg Collection:
	Violet Hunt (Mrs. Hueffer)
	Edward Marsh
	Virginia Woolf
NYP-RL	New York Public Library, Research Libraries:
	Donald B. Clark
	David Greenhood
	Eugene Saxton
UCL:	University of Chicago, Joseph Regenstein Library:
	Harriet Monroe
UL-BC	University of Leeds, Brotherton Collection:
	Clement King Shorter
UT-HRC	University of Texas at Austin, Humanities Research Center:
	Edmund Blunden
	Christopher Morley
	Mrs. Marie Belloc-Lowndes
	P.E.N.
	Idella Purnell Stone
	Geoffrey Harry Wells (Geoffrey West)

Notes and References

Preface

1. Ida A. Wylie, *My Life with George: an Unconventional Autobiography* (New York: Random House, 1940), p. 266.
2. See Jerome H. Buckley's *Victorian Temper: A Study in Literary Culture* (New York, 1951), especially Chapter 1, for a discussion of the contradictions included in the assumptions about Victorianism.
3. R. Ellis Roberts, *Portrait of Stella Benson* (London: Macmillan Co., 1939), p. 325; hereafter cited as Roberts, *Portrait*.

Chapter One

1. Roberts, *Portrait*, p. 30. This is the only published biography of Stella Benson, but its aim is to give an impression of the writer, not a complete history. Therefore, although this is the source of much of the general biographical material that follows, this chapter is *not* a summary of Roberts's work but a biography drawn from his *Portrait*, other published material, and unpublished letters.
2. Stella Benson, "Another Tyranny," *Bookman* 48 (1919):643.
3. Stella Benson, "Bags and Barrows," *Dial* 67 (1919):12.
4. Stella Benson, "Little Back Room," *Dial* 67, (October 4, 1919):294.
5. Stella Benson, "Bags and Barrows," *Dial* 67 (1919):14.
6. Harriet Monroe, "News Notes," *Poetry: A Magazine of Verse* 43 (1934): 292.
7. Unpublished letter to Harriet Monroe dated 11-15-18, courtesy of Joseph Regenstein Library, University of Chicago. Hereafter unpublished letters (UPL) will be cited by library code, name of addressee, and date, as UPL: UCL, Monroe 11-15-18. For explanation of library code see Appendix.
8. Roberts, *Portrait*, p. 70.
9. Ibid., p. 72.
10. UPL: HL, Bynner 12-3-19.
11. UPL: LC, Bender 8-14(23?).
12. UPL: HL, Bynner n.d. (summer 1919?).
13. UPL: UCL, Monroe 12-12-18; UPL: HL, Lowell 10-14-18.
14. Roberts, *Portrait*, p. 55.
15. Ibid., p. 21.
16. UPL: HL, Bynner 2-21-19.
17. Wylie, *My Life with George*, p. 23.
18. Roberts, *Portrait*, p. 88.
19. UPL: MCL, Bender 4-14-23.
20. Stella Benson, "Lines Written in a Temper," *Saturday Review of Literature*, September 25, 1926, p. 54.

21. UPL: BM, Schiff 3-2-25.
22. Roberts, *Portrait*, pp. 147–48, 132.
23. Stella Benson, "Reflections in a Mirror," *Saturday Review of Literature*, August 15, 1931, p. 54.
24. Roberts, *Portrait*, pp. 123–24.
25. UPL: LC, Bender 4-12-25.
26. UPL: BM, Schiff 4-28-25.
27. UPL: UT-HRC, Wells 7-8-24; UPL: LC, Bender 3-15-25.
28. UPL: BM, Schiff 7-29-25.
29. Ibid., 1-4-26.
30. UPL: NYP-RL, Clark 8-8-27.
31. UPL: HL, Bynner 12-27-25.
32. UPL: BM, Schiff 1-4-26.
33. Roberts, *Portrait*, pp. 176, 188.
34. Ibid., p. 205.
35. Ibid., p. 215.
36. UPL: MB, Schiff 4-14-30.
37. UPL: NYP-RL, Clark 2-15-31.
38. Roberts, *Portrait*, p. 263.
39. UPL: BM, Schiff 8-2-31.
40. UPL: MCL, Bender 9-11-(31?).
41. UPL: NYP-RL, Clark 2-27-32.
42. UPL: NYP-B, Woolf 6-6-33.
43. Roberts, *Portrait*, p. 249.
44. UPL: LC, Bender 1-1-33.
45. Roberts, *Portrait*, p. 297.

Chapter Two

1. Stella Benson, *Goodbye, Stranger* (London, 1926), p. 196.
2. Stella Benson, *I Pose* (New York, 1916), p. 65.
3. Ibid., p. 141.
4. Stella Benson, *Tobit Transplanted* (London, 1931), pp. 90, 92.
5. UPL: BM, Schiff 3-26-25.

Chapter Three

1. Stella Benson, *I Pose* (New York, 1916), pp. 1, 22–23; hereafter cited in the text as *IP* followed by page number.
2. E. M. Forster, *Aspects of the Novel* (New York, 1927), p. 55.
3. *Nation*, February 24, 1916, p. 25.

Chapter Four

1. John A. Lester, *Journey Through Despair 1880–1914: Transformations in British Literary Culture* (Princeton, 1968), p. 114.

2. *Dial*, August 16, 1917, p. 117.
3. Stella Benson, *This Is the End* (London, 1917), p. 10; hereafter cited in the text as *TITE* followed by page number.
4. W. H. Boynton, "Some Stories of the Month," *Bookman*, July 1917, p. 533.
5. Stella Benson, *Living Alone* (London, 1919), p. 77; hereafter cited in the text as *LA* followed by page number.

Chapter Five

1. When Stella Benson died in 1933 she left unfinished a novel which she referred to as △ ▽. In spite of her request that no incomplete work be published posthumously, Benson's husband published the fragment under the title *Mundos* (London: Macmillan and Co., 1935). The narrative ends with a kidnapping and leaves a murder victim undiscovered, a murderer at large, and a dwarf marooned on a cliff.
2. UPL: UT-HRC, Wells 7-8-24.
3. John Gawsworth, *Ten Contemporaries: Notes Toward Their Definitive Bibliography* (London, 1933), p. 40.
4. Stella Benson, *The Poor Man* (London, 1922), p. 244; hereafter cited in the text as *PM* followed by page number.
5. Roberts, *Portrait*, p. 115.
6. UPL: BM, Schiff 3-12-25.
7. Stella Benson, *Pipers and a Dancer* (New York, 1924), p. 175; hereafter cited in the text as *PD* followed by page number.
8. *Times Literary Supplement* (London), October 2, 1924, p. 610.
9. Roberts, *Portrait*, p. 136.

Chapter Six

1. William C. Frierson, *The English Novel in Transition 1885−1940* (Norman, Oklahoma, 1942), p. 247.
2. *Times Literary Supplement* (London), December 9, 1926, p. 908.
3. Stella Benson, *Goodbye, Stranger* (London, 1926), p. 297; hereafter cited in the text as *GS* followed by page number.
4. Gawsworth, *Ten Contemporaries*, p. 40.
5. L. P. Hartley, *Saturday Review*, December 11, 1926, p. 737.
6. Ibid., p. 737.
7. UPL: LC, Bender 9-29-26.
8. Stella Benson, *Tobit Transplanted* (London, 1931), p. 38; hereafter cited in the text as *TT* followed by page number.

Chapter Seven

1. Stella Benson, *Pull Devil, Pull Baker* (New York, 1933), p. ix; hereafter cited in the text as *PD, PB* followed by page number.

2. Stella Benson, *Collected Short Stories* (London, 1936), p. 54; hereafter cited in the text as *CSS* followed by page number.

3. Stella Benson, *Worlds Within Worlds* (London, 1928), p. 8; hereafter cited in the text as *WWW* followed by page number.

4. Stella Benson, *The Little World* (London, 1925), p. 37; hereafter cited in the text as *LW* followed by page number.

Chapter Eight

1. David Daiches, *The Present Age in British Literature* (Bloomington: Indiana University Press, 1958), p. 284.

Selected Bibliography

PRIMARY SOURCES

1. Novels:
Far-Away Bride. New York: Press of the Readers Club, 1941. (New York: Harper & Brothers, 1930; English title, *Tobit Transplanted.* London: Macmillan & Co., 1931.)
Goodbye, Stranger. London: Macmillan & Co., 1926.
I Pose. New York: Macmillan Co., 1916.
Living Alone. London: Macmillan & Co., 1919.
Mundos: An Unfinished Novel. London: Macmillan & Co., 1935.
Pipers and a Dancer. New York: Macmillan Co., 1924.
Poor Man. London: Macmillan & Co., 1922.
This Is the End. London: Macmillan & Co., 1917.

2. Collected Poems, Short Stories, and Articles:
Christmas Formula and Other Stories. London: Joiner & Steele, 1932.
Collected Short Stories. London: Macmillan & Co., 1936.
Little World. London: Macmillan & Co., 1925.
Pull Devil, Pull Baker. (with Count Nicolas de Toulouse Lautrec de Savine, K.M.) New York: Harper & Brothers, 1933.
Twenty. London: Macmillan & Co., 1918.
Worlds Within Worlds. London: Macmillan & Co., 1929.

3. Uncollected Short Stories:
"Destination." *Harper's Monthly Magazine* 164 (December 1931):23−28.
"Dream." *Saturday Review of Literature,* April 19, 1930, p. 946.
"Nicholas the Debonair." *Fortnightly Review* 139 (1933):77−89.
"Prank." *Scholastic,* January 8, 1938, pp. 3−4.
"Search for Mr. Loo." *Harper's Monthly Magazine* 162 (May 1931):653−59.
"Two Ghosts." *Harper's Monthly Magazine* 161 (August 1930):371−72.

4. Uncollected Articles:
"Alarums and Excursions." *Fortnightly Review* 134 (1930):625−34.
"Another Tyranny." *Bookman* 48 (1919):640−43.
"Bags and Barrows." *Dial,* July 12, 1919, pp. 11−14.
"Blaming the Shrew." *Saturday Review of Literature,* September 1, 1934, p. 83.
"Den-Fil—Useful Knowledge." *Saturday Review of Literature,* May 28, 1932, pp. 753−54.

"Detour in Tonkin." *Fortnightly Review* 141 (1934):77−85.
"Eleuthera." *Saturday Review of Literature*, May 4, 1929, p. 974.
"Escape from Adventure." *Fortnightly Review* 129 (1928):277−82.
"Firefly to Steer By." *Harper's Monthly Magazine* 166 (December 1932):122−24.
"Freudian America." *Bookman* 49 (1919):304−05.
"Hunting Worlds." *Bookman* 53 (1921):344−45.
"Ignoramus as Gardener in the Far East." *Fortnightly Review* 136 (1931): 478−81.
"Lines Written in a Temper." *Saturday Review of Literature*, September 25, 1926, pp. 134−35.
"Little Back Room." *Dial*, October 4, 1919, pp. 291−94.
"More Dreams." *Saturday Review of Literature*, December 16, 1933, p. 354.
"Observations on Canine Blue Blood." *Harper's Monthly Magazine* 167 (August 1933):375−78.
"Reflection in a Mirror." *Saturday Review of Literature*, August 15, 1931, p. 54.
"Watching Lips Moving." *Saturday Review of Literature*, June 20, 1931, p. 910.
"Wild Pygmies Afloat." *Harper's Monthly Magazine* 166 (May 1933):735−39.

5. Unpublished Material:

Austin, Texas. University of Texas, Humanities Research Center: 2 letters to Edmund Blunden; 2 letters to Mrs. Marie Belloc-Lowndes; 4 letters to Christopher Morley; 2 letters to Idella Purnell Stone; 2 letters to Geoffrey Harry Wells.

Cambridge, Mass. Harvard University Library: 1 letter to Albert Bender; 21 letters to Witter Bynner; 3 letters to Amy Lowell; 1 MS poem, "To remind you of Berkeley Hills."

Chicago, Ill. University of Chicago, Joseph Regenstein Library: 4 letters to Harriet Monroe; 1 MS poem, "If you were careless."

Leeds, England. University of Leeds, Brotherton Library: 3 letters to Clement King Shorter.

Liverpool, England. University of Liverpool, Harold Cohen Library: 1 letter to A. K. Bully.

London, England. British Museum Library: 27 letters to Stephen Hudson (Sidney Schiff).

New York, N. Y. New York Public Library, Berg Collection: 1 letter to Violet Hunt; 2 letters to Edward March; 3 letters to Virginia Woolf.

―――. New York Public Library, Research Libraries: 22 letters to Donald B. Clark (with a preface to the letters by Clark); 4 letters to David Greenhood; 4 letters to Eugene Saxton.

Oakland, Calif. Mills College, Library: 27 letters to Albert Bender; 1 MS poem, "To Albert."

Washington, D. C. Library of Congress: letters to Albert Bender.

SECONDARY SOURCES

General

Forster, E. M. *Aspects of the Novel.* New York: Harcourt, Brace, & World, Inc., 1927. Does not consider Benson, but interesting as statement by an author to whom Benson invited comparison.

Frierson, William C. *The English Novel in Transition 1885—1940.* Norman: University of Oklahoma Press, 1942.

Kaplan, Sydney Janet. *Feminine Consciousness in the Modern British Novel.* Chicago: University of Illinois Press, 1975. Analysis of the development of a feminine consciousness in literary characters.

Lester, John A., Jr. *Journey through Despair 1880—1914: Transformations in British Literary Culture.* Princeton: Princeton University Press, 1968. Perceptive discussion of the spirit of an age revealed in literature.

Miles, Rosalind. *The Fiction of Sex.* New York: Barnes and Noble, 1974. Valuable discussion of the themes and significance of sex differences in the modern novel.

Rogers, Katherine M. *The Troublesome Helpmate: A History of Misogyny in Literature.* Seattle: University of Washington Press, 1966. Chronological discussion of misogyny in English and American Literature.

Spacks, Patricia Meyer. *The Female Imagination.* New York: Alfred A. Knopf, 1975. Intended as anti-historical and apolitical examination of themes developed by women in literature written in English.

Stubbs, Patricia. *Women and Fiction: Feminism and the Novel 1880—1920.* Sussex: Harvester Press, 1979. Explores the transformation of the feminine ideal in the novel, concludes there has been little significant change.

Biographical and Critical

Battiscombe, Georgina. "Stella Benson." *Nineteenth Century* 141 (1947): 208—16. General discussion concluding that *Tobit Transplanted* is a "small masterpiece," earlier work entertaining but not as good because too much self-revelation. Compares Benson favorably with Katherine Mansfield.

Bottome, Phyllis. *Stella Benson.* San Francisco: Grabhorn Press, 1934. Privately printed personal appreciation.

Brittain, Vera. *Testament of Friendship.* London: MacMillan & Co., 1942. Brief references to Stella Benson.

Collins, Joseph A. "Two Lesser Literary Ladies of London: Stella Benson and Virginia Woolf." In *The Doctor Looks at Literature: Psychological Studies of Life and Letters.* New York: George H. Doran Co., 1923. Praises first four novels.

Daiches, David. *The Present Age in British Literature.* Bloomington: Indiana University Press, 1958. Brief observation that she is underrated.

Dictionary of National Biography 1931–1940. Edited by L. G. Wickham Legg. London: Oxford University Press, 1949. Biographical summary.

Gawsworth, J. *Ten Contemporaries: Notes Toward Their Definitive Bibliography.* London: Joiner & Steele, 1933. Includes Benson's comments about her work, then a descriptive bibliography of her books.

Johnson, Reginald Brinkley. "Stella Benson" In *Some Contemporary Novelists (Women).* London: Leonard Parsons, 1920; rpt. Freeport, N.Y.: Essay Index Reprint Series, Books for Libraries Press, 1970. Praises her realism, mysticism, and dramatic sense in her first three novels.

Kunitz, Stanley J. and Haycraft, Howard. *Twentieth Century Authors: A Biographical Dictionary of Modern Literature.* New York: W. H. Wilson Co., 1942. Biographical summary.

Mais, Stuart P. B. "Stella Benson." In *Some Modern Authors.* New York: Dodd, Mead 1923; rpt. Freeport, N.Y.: Essay Index Reprint Series, Books for Libraries Press, 1970. An extended plot summary of *The Poor Man* concluded with praise for Benson's study of inferiority complex.

Mellers, W. H. "Fairies in Bloomsbohemia." *Scrutiny* 8 (September 1939): 221–25. Ostensibly a review of *Portrait of Stella Benson*, actually an attempt to place Benson's achievement. Perplexed by high praise of Benson, Mellers judges her a "sociological specimen" inadequate as an artist because of her failure of belief.

Monroe, Harriet. "New Notes." *Poetry: A Magazine of Verse* 43 (February 1934):292–93. Brief comment on Benson's appearance in Chicago in 1918.

Morley, Christopher. *The Powder of Sympathy.* New York: Doubleday, Page & Co., 1923.

———. "Stella Benson." *Saturday Review of Literature*, December 16, 1933, p. 354.

"Obituary." *Publishers Weekly*, December 16, 1933, p. 2083.

"Obituary." *The Times* (London), December 8, 1933.

Roberts, R. Ellis. *Portrait of Stella Benson.* London: Macmillan Co., 1939. Biography with appreciative but condescending critical commentary. The only book about Stella Benson to date.

Seymour-Smith, Martin. *Who's Who in Twentieth Century Literature.* New York: McGraw Hill, 1976. Brief identification; looks forward to Benson's diaries.

Woolf, Virginia. *A Writer's Diary: Being Extracts from the Diary of Virginia Woolf.* Edited by Leonard Woolf. London: Hogarth Press, 1954. Brief comment at news of Stella Benson's death.

———. *The Letters of Virginia Woolf.* Vols. 3, 4, 5. Edited by Nigel Nicholsen and Joanne Trautmann. New York: Harcourt Brace Jovanovich, 1979. Scattered observations on Benson and her writing.

Wylie, Ida A. R. *My Life with George: An Unconventional Autobiography.* New York: Random House, 1940. Brief description of Benson in California, 1919.

Book Reviews

I Pose, 1915.
  Kelley, Florence Finch. "Firstlings in Fiction." *Bookman* 43 (May 1916): 325.
  Nation, February 24, 1916, p. 225.
This Is the End, 1917.
  Boynton, H. W. "Some Stories of the Month." *Bookman*, July 1917, p. 533.
  Dial, August 16, 1917, p. 117.
  Nation, June 21, 1917, p. 737.
Twenty, 1918.
  Walsh, Thomas. "Poets, Rose Fever, and other Seasonal Manifestations" *Bookman* 47 (August 1918):643.
  Dial, December 14, 1918, p. 574.
The Poor Man, 1922.
  International Book Reviews. October 1923, p. 67.
  New Republic, September 12, 1923, p. 81.
Pipers and a Dancer, 1924.
  Holden, Raymond. "Stella Benson's Latest." *Saturday Review of Literature*, October 25, 1924, p. 223.
The Little World, 1925.
  Niles, Blair. "The Travel Diary of a Novelist." *Bookman* 62 (October 1925):211–13.
Goodbye, Stranger, 1926.
  Nation, December 29, 1926, p. 696.
  New Republic, December 1, 1926, p. 49.
  Saturday Review, December 11, 1926, p. 737.
  Times Literary Supplement (London), December 9, 1926, p. 908.
Worlds Within Worlds, 1928.
  Saturday Review of Literature, April 6, 1929, p. 850.
  Saturday Review of Politics, Literature, Science and Art, December 8, 1928, p. 772.
  Times Literary Supplement (London), December 6, 1928, p. 956.
The Far-Away Bride, 1930 (*Tobit Transplanted*, 1931 in England).
  New York Herald Tribune. November 16, 1930, pp. 1, 4.
  Saturday Review of Literature, December 6, 1930, p. 415.
Pull Devil, Pull Baker, 1933.
  Nation, August 2, 1933, p. 136.

New Republic, October 11, 1933, p. 258.
New York Herald Tribune: Books, July 2, 1933, p. 1.
New York Times, July 2, 1933, p. 4.
Saturday Review of Literature, July 1, 1933, p. 674.
Saturday Review of Politics, Literature, Science and Art, April 15, 1933, p. 365.
Times Literary Supplement (London), April 13, 1933, p. 259.

Mundos, 1935.
New Statesman and Nation, April 27, 1935, p. 594.

Index

Apocrypha, 12, 85, 97, 100
Anderson, Shaemas (James) O'Gorman, 7
Anderson, Stella. *See* Benson, Stella
Auden, W.H., 19
Austen, Jane, 11; *Emma*, 50; *Pride and Prejudice*, 93

Barrie, J.M., 18
Benson, A.C., 97
Benson, Stella, biography of, *1–15*, 62, 72; poetry, 22; short stories, 22

    WORKS:
"Cornishman, The," 118
"Christmas, 1917," 117
Poems, 117
"To Him that Hath . . . ," 117
Twenty, 3

    NON-FICTION PROSE:
Little World, The, 10, 118, 120
World Within Worlds, 118, 119

    NOVELS:
Goodbye, Stranger, 10, 17, 60, *85–97*, 105, 123
I Pose, 3, 16, *24–39*, 40, 55, 67, 83, 84, 105, 123
Living Alone, 40, *53–61*, 67, 68, 105, 108, 123
Pipers and a Dancer, 10, 16, 62, *72–84*, 91, 109, 123
Poor Man, The, 7, 8, 10, 11, 16, *62–72*, 91, 104, 108, 123

This is the End, 3, 16, *40–53*, 55, 67, 68, 84, 108, 109, 123
Tobit Transplanted (Am. ed. *The Far Away Bride*), 12, 13, 14, 20, 21, 22, 85, *97–110*, 123

    SHORT STORIES:
"Angelina," 112
Awakening, The, 111
Christmas Formula and Other Stories, 111
Collected Short Stories, 111, *113–17*
"Desert Islander, The," 115
"Dream, A," 113
"Hope Against Hope," 114
Hope Against Hope and Other Stories, 111
"Lili, the Noty Gerl," 112
"Man Who Fell in Love with the Cooperative Stores, The," 112
Man Who Missed the Bus, The, 111
Pull Devil, Pull Baker, 111–13
"Story Coldly Told," 116
"Submarine," 115

Brittain, Vera, 125
Bynner, Witter, 6
Byron, George Gordon Lord, 77

characterization, 17, 43, 45, 60, 68, 123
Chesterton, G.K., 18
color imagery, 35–39; blue, 35–37, 39, 105; gray, 35–36, 38–39, 105; red, 35–38, 105; yellow, 35, 38, 39

communication, 12, 15, 56, 57, 60, 61, 102, 117, 120
Conrad, Joseph, *Jude the Obscure*, 18

Daiches, David, 122
de la Mare, Walter, 85; "Listeners," 18
de Stael, Mme, *De l'influence des passions*, 77
Dial, 40
Dickens, Charles, 21
DuMaurier, Daphne, *Rebecca*, 50

Eliot, George, *Middlemarch*, 50
Eliot, T.S., "Prufrock," 69; "Waste Land, The," 18, 19

fantasy, 18, 47, 51, 53, 55, 59, 60, 61, 89, 97
feminist, 21
Forster, E.M., 25
Frierson, William, 85
frigidity, 101

Greene, Graham, 121; *The Heart of the Matter*, 54

Hardy, Thomas, 18
Harlequin books, 50
heroines, 21, 22, 55, 66, 75, 87, 104
Holtby, Winifred, 125
homosexuality, 75, 79
Huxley, Aldous, *Those Barren Leaves*, 23

imagery, 21; *See also* 35–39
identity, 22, 24, 31–35, 39, 75, 77, 78, 81, 84, 87, 90–94
individuality, 61, 84, 99, 121
irony, 19, 21, 43, 44, 47, 61, 63, 67, 100
isolation, 21, 23, 39, 46, 49, 52, 55, 57, 59, 60, 61, 84, 85, 92, 94, 96, 99, 102, 103, 107, 120

James, Henry, *The Bostonians*, 75
Johnson, Reginald, 124
Joyce, James, *Ulysses*, 16

Kaye-Smith, Sheila, 125
Keats, John, "Ode to a Nightingale," 53
Kipling, Rudyard, 41

Lawrence, D.H., 18, 22, 79
Lester, John A., 40
loneliness, 19, 51, 54, 55, 57, 62, 102, 122
Lowell, Amy, 5

Macaulay, Rose, 125
marriage, 49, 50, 59, 90, 75, 77, 88, 94, 99, 108, 109
men, 21, 22, 50, 60, 66, 106
Monroe, Harriet, 4, 5
Morley, Christopher, 125
Murdoch, Iris, 22

Nation, 31
narration, method of, 43, 62, 70, 111, 123; *See also*: point of view

P.E.N. Club, 14
pity, 17, 99, 106, 108
point of view, 16, 17, 119; *See also*: method of narration
Pope, Bertha, 4
pose, 24, 28, 69; *See also*: identity; *also* individuality; *also* roles

Rebecca of Sunnybrook Farm, 50
Richardson, Dorothy, *Pilgrimage*, 16
Roberts, Ellis, 6, 82
roles, men's, 83, 91, 94
roles, women's, 22, 59, 91, 94, 97, 104, 106; *See also* women's sphere
Romantic tradition, 90
romantic values, 18, 54, 55

Saturday Review, 89
Schiff, Sidney, 14, 72
Seymour-Smith, Martin, *Who's Who in Twentieth Century Literature*, 124
sentimental, 45, 117
sentimentality, 33, 55, 65, 66, 93, 111, 118
sexual matters, 22, 66, 80, 88, 89, 91, 101, 102
Sinclair, May, 16, 22
Spacks, Patricia, *The Female Imagination*, 90
stream of consciousness, 16, 17, 18

Thackeray, W.M., *Vanity Fair*, 16
Times, The (London), 74, 85

understatement, 19, 100

Vie Heureuse Prize, 12, 97

Waugh, Evelyn, 21
West, Rebecca, 121
Wilde, Oscar, 34
women's sphere, 19, 21, 22, 24, 26, 31–35, 39, 50, 66, 75, 76, 78, 81, 83, 87, 88
Woolf, Virginia, 15, 87; *Orlando*, 18
Wylie, Elinor, 125
Wylie, Ida A., 6

Yeats, William Butler, "Easter 1916," 43